BALANCING THE SIX WHEELS OF SUCCESS

M. Harihara Mahadevan

INDIA • SINGAPORE • MALAYSIA

ISBN 979-8-89026-742-9

Samarpanam

This book is dedicated to my Parents, who brought me to this World for a Purpose, to my maternal grandpa who was instrumental for my graduation and to all my Gurus, who transformed me from nowhere to somewhere

Contents

Foreword from SPIC Top Executive

I had the good fortune to read the book by Hariharamahadevan titled *"Live with Bliss and Peace"*. I have known him for many decades in different avatars namely a colleague, a trainer, a motivational speaker and now a writer. I have always been attracted by his thoughts on leading a righteous life which ultimately results in inner calm and happiness. These thoughts are beautifully captured in his latest book, *Live with Bliss and Peace.* The serious and somewhat complicated concepts are explained in a very simple and interesting narration so that readers of all ages can easily understand. The author resorts to stories, anecdotes, real life incidences and examples to illustrate these principles while elaborating them graphically, pictographically and through commonly used words.

All debates on ways of living will end with an undeniable fact that the human beings want a life with *bliss and peace.* The author identifies six most important factors which *together* help one to achieve these objectives. The six chapters of this book deal with these six factors, namely, physical wellness, mental wellness, family wellness, career wellness, social wellness and spiritual wellness.

As one begins reading the book, one is stuck with the bold statement *"your life partner is not your spouse, but your body"*. The author, then goes on to explain about fourteen medicines which are not available in medical shops; but are freely available through our choice to keep us physically fit.

The story of a non-existent goat beautifully brings out the fact we spoil the mental health worrying about issues that do not exist.

Thoughts, indeed, lead to 'destiny' and the readers are made to understand this through very interesting narrations.

Like in all contracts where there is *letter & spirit*, similarly in all communications, the author argues that there is *meaning & feeling*. Relationship is built on two strokes (responses) both positive and negative and the author explains this with an interesting *"90/10 Made for Each Other story"*. The importance of the support of family (friends circle) for all generations, while facing success and failure, is well brought out.

Money is important and career is the best way to earn it. Success in career depends on passion, effort, perseverance and focus. The author brings out this aspect in a very forceful manner through several practical examples.

The author sums up the purpose of our living in two profound statements; "it is in giving that we receive" and "service to humanity is the best work of life". He goes on to argue with fictional examples how 'giving to society' and 'serving the society' lead to everlasting happiness.

Mere efforts without righteousness and with ego do not bring results, so explains the author. He gives this very simple meaning to spiritualism. The feelings I had when I finished the book were complete humbleness and humility.

The essence of a good life leading to bliss and peace is the way we balance these six wellness factors which the author calls as 'wheels'.

It is difficult to stay away from religion in any book on philosophy of life; but Hariharamahadevan has done this wonderfully while using examples of God Almighty and those from scriptures in a generic way. Best Wishes to him.

S. R. Ramakrishnan

Whole Time Director, SPIC Ltd

Foreword from MD & CEO - South Indian Bank

I am quite fortunate to know the author Harihara Mahadevan during my formative years in work life at SPIC, Tuticorin, as an established, dedicated professional and as a Jaycee leader and trainer who identified and developed many future leaders. He had transformed into a highly successful life coach with his unique one on one interactions that carry no traces of selfish motive. That fact is evident in this fabulous book. This master piece is a wonderful output from a great human being, who truly believes in making the world a better place. My humble salute to my senior, friend and my well-wisher.

Hari's interests towards understanding what a successful life, is quite evident in giving equal attention to other aspects of life apart from professional wellness. Hari is a very practical individual and a keen observer of events happening around him. This book, for which I had the fortune of writing this foreword, brings out the complete aspect of `wellness' across different facets of one's life. As we look around in society, where there is so much of imbalance in many so called `successful' people, the key aspects of what actually is `success' have been well brought out in this master piece, through well-choreographed topics covering the entire gamut of one's life. If one carefully looks at the aspects covered, they have been so well chosen that any of them found missing can make life so less fulfilling. We have enough case studies, where we have heard people trading health for money and in their later years, trade money to get health and often unsuccessfully. This aspect of Physical wellness has been very assertively emphasized.

Mental wellness is so integral to the success of the individual as the balance, a person brings out, while dealing with the positives and negatives of events happening around him. The so called wealthy nations in western world reports, many suffering from some form of mental illness. The maximum sale of medicines to cure mental illness happen in the so called western countries, which claim material wealth and an outstanding infrastructure to provide high quality of life. The significance of this wellness has been well covered in this book.

Family wellness is quite evident when we look at certain societies particularly in the eastern countries like China, India etc. Often in these countries, the support an individual gets from their family is immense and that indeed enables them face adversities or challenges in life with ease. We see this aspect quite contrary in so called advanced civilisation of Western countries. An individual, who is aspiring to be successful should focus on family wellness without which, the fundamental blocks of building a good family with well nurtured children, who would then play a meaningful role in their life will be missed. This has been described so well in this book.

Regarding career wellness, there are two dimensions in my view. One is how well do we balance work and life. The second aspect is how well we handle the vicissitudes of work environment. In my long career spanning more than 3 decades, I have often found the skillsets and the attitudes needed to lead a successful job vary, as one goes up the career ladder. There have been many instances, where individuals have moved up through fast track but not fully equipped with the skillsets needed to handle a responsible senior position. On the contrary, we have often found an extremely talented individual in their functional area suffering due to inadequate skill sets in the Emotional balance. Hari had dealt with the IQ, EQ etc., so well in this book and I believe, it will be extremely useful for professionals of all ages.

Social wellness is often the less taught and less understood in any academic curriculum. The positive development across the world is in recognising this aspect to be an important part of any successful individual or a leader. The apt examples given in this book demonstrate that aspect very well.

Spiritual wellness is the most basic but often the most neglected one. This wellness is probably the most important aspect, to make one realise their true nature by virtue of the awareness they get in going through the complexities of life. If this is ignored, eventually, the unanswered questions of life events can trigger so much of negative tendencies leading to dejected, unhappy existence. We do come across individuals, who have everything life has to offer but found to be quite hollow, as they don't have happiness in their existence. Am so happy that Hari had covered this most important `wellness' as part of Blissful life, as this is truly the most needed, to even appreciate Blissfulness.

In nutshell, the timing of this book by Hari is so appropriate, as we are in the midst of mega changes in the eco system. On one hand, we have the best of knowledge available at the stroke of button from multifarious sources, equally, we are just a few minutes away from the planet going to ashes with so many nuclear missiles in the hands of few countries, who are at loggerheads all the time. At an individual level, we have the best of luxury, the humanity had ever seen and equally, we experience chaotic impact at the physical and mental level for every human being. Hari indeed had addressed the essence of life which is to live in peace and bliss, which is possible only when an individual shape themselves with the balanced aspect of the various wellnesses, he has covered so beautifully in this masterpiece.

Murali Ramakrishnan

MD & CEO – South Indian Bank

Foreword from Director, Tamerica TV

It is my pleasure to give my foreword to the book "LIVE WITH BLISS & PEACE" written by Harihara Mahadeven which focuses on the balancing of six wheels of life – Physical, Mental, Family, Career, Social, and Spiritual.

As the founder of TamericaTV, the first Tamil channel from the USA, I have seen the importance of addressing the various aspects of life, that contribute to our overall well-being.

The author has done an excellent job of distilling complex ideas into a simple framework, that is easy to understand and implement. The six wheels of life serve as a reminder that our lives are multifaceted and neglecting any one aspect can have a negative impact on our overall happiness.

The practical tips and exercises provided in this book, are sure to help readers achieve balance and lead a more fulfilling life. Whether you are struggling to find meaning and purpose, or simply looking to improve your relationships or career, this book has something for everyone.

I am delighted to see this program that was initially streamed on Tamerica TV, now being transformed into a book. The fact that it is being published by Notion Press, is a testament to the quality of the content and its potential to make a positive impact on the lives of readers.

I highly recommend this book to anyone who is looking to improve the quality of life and find more joy and meaning in his/her everyday experiences. Congratulations to the author, Harihara Mahadeven on a job well done. I wish all readers the best of luck on their journey towards bliss and peace.

Mahesh Nattanmai

Founder, TamericaTV.

Accolades for the Book

All the chapters in the book are weaved through anecdotes and stories that every reader can relate to life to progress and prosper. Illustrated appropriately with diagrams, the conceptualization of concepts are made convenient and comfortable. A great service to mankind, Hari sir has bundled his years of wisdom into 6 easily understandable yet very effective tool kit for life.

– Srinivasan

www.peoplepoint.biz

www.trekoneacademy.com

The book aptly classified by my close friend and Motivator, Hari, as six areas of wellness will surely serve as an inspiring guide for the readers to think, analyse and apply the concepts in their lives.

– A. V. Ramanathan

Trainer, Former Head (HRD), Heavy water Board, DAE

I know the author Mr Harihara mahadevan since 1986. Since then his growth has been phenomenal in all walks of life. This book is a tool that will transform many who are groping in the dark and march ahead towards a bright future in all the six spheres of life.

– M. Chidambaram International Trainer

I have known Mr. Harihara Mahadevan for many years and his enthusiasm and dedication and most of all his positive spirit is extremely commendable. I wish him all the very best for his publication which is truly enlivening and inspiring

– Capt. Ajay Gangadharan, Captain Superintendent,
Maritime Foundation, Chennai

Numerous stories and real life examples would attract readership which I personally enjoyed. It also gave a feel that I am not just reading one book but got the essence of multiple books-excellent transition to the core message from the stories or real life examples. A simple language usage made it comfortable reading as a non native English speaker and would help young kids.

– Sivakumar Nadarajan
Head of competency,
Rolls-Royce Singapore

While at a glance, one thinks that the 6 wellnesses described are dependent, on a deeper level, I realize that these are truly six degrees of freedom one could exercise to have a well rounded, grounded and successful life. The balance would be based on the need of the stages of life one is in. The examples and conversations are quite relatable and references also show that the quest to conquer these 6 wellnesses are universal. A read to ponder and take away.

– Suba Viswanathan Senior Engineering
Programme Manager, Honeywell Aerospace USA

Harihara Mahadevan, it is clear from his ex-colleague's beautiful foreword, has worn many hats. But I always wish to remember him as a writer, whether in English or in Tamil. He is never far away from his favourite craft, ' full of that energy that collects, combines, amplifies and animates'. I have known him for more than five decades. He is a happy parent, reliable friend, a loving husband (he lost his wife early), dutiful son, and above all, an admirable human being. He is sure to make waves with his latest book, ***Live with Bliss and Peace***.

His upbringing and early training have enabled him to adopt a down-to-earth approach to problem-solving whether in the family or in industry'. He seems to believe with Johnson that " the task of the present writers requires, together with the learning which is to be gained from books, that experience which can never be attained by solitary diligence, but must arise from generous converse and accurate observation of the real world".

In his latest book, Mr Mahadevan discusses the complexity of life, duties cast on humans at various times and in different situations and the loss of centrality of human beings in this mysterious universe. This is what an American writer would call a companionable book.

I wish Harihara Mahadevan success in his mission of service

– K.S. Mahadevan Senior News Editor (Retired)
Indian Express

Preface

The book you now hold in your hands grew out of a two-day training program for corporates, **Live with Bliss and Peace,** which I hosted in 2012 and was well-received. My earnest wish to reach a wider audience across the world was fulfilled through a webinar in English of the same topic with 62 episodes. Thanks to the efforts of Mrs. Amutha Sargurunathan, who is like my daughter, and GR P.G. Rajan, my close friend and well-wisher and founder of 1234 Foundation. Mrs Amutha's suggestion that the program be conducted as a webinar was readily accepted by Mr Mahesh Nattanmai, Director of Tamerica, the only Tamil Channel of the US.

It is my sincere hope and prayer that this book will spread my message to a still wider audience. I thank the Notion Press, publishers of this work, for their expertise and co-operation.

I would be failing in my duty if I did not express my thanks to my copy editor, Mrs. Shanthi Thiraviyam. Retired English Professor from Madurai, who read the draft through and made useful suggestions. I take this opportunity to thank two other well-wishers, Dr (Prof) Gurumoorthy, Mr A V Ramanathan, whose suggestions have helped improve the draft.

My profuse thanks to Mr S.R. Ramakrishnan, Whole Time Director of M/S SPIC LTD, Mr. Murali Ramakrishnan, MD and CEO of South Indian Bank and Mr Mahesh Nattanmai for their forewords to the book. I acknowledge my debt of gratitude to all my well-wishers, including those few whose names may have been inadvertently missed.

I extend my sincerest gratitude to Infinithoughts magazine for publishing my articles in 2017, from which I have incorporated selected portions into this book.

The entire proceeds of this book will go to charity. Please read, benefit and recommend to your circles.

M. Harihara Mahadevan

Kanchipuram

M-9841356075

Prelude to the Book

- *A prominent business man in south of Tamil Nadu was amassing wealth, without an iota of care for his health. At the age of 45, he suddenly collapsed due to cardiac arrest.*
- *A friend of mine, with three Ph.D in Chemistry had deserted his family, because of his liquor addiction and by his premature death at early 50s.*
- *A very famous person in Chennai, who produced many IAS committed suicide.*

These are some of the recent news items that affected me very much.

What is the root cause of all these and what can be the possible solutions? – ***These kinds of questions have been reverberating of late in my mind.***

Many are unconsciously becoming the victims, to their own self imposed traps like:-

- *Buying anger, resulting in buying unwanted acidity*
- *Buying jealousy, leading to undesired headache*
- *Getting into hatred, the by product of which is ulcer*
- *Involving in excessive stressful activities, inviting blood pressure*

How can they avoid those traps?

Technology might have done wonders, brought people together virtually. But it has separated them in their hearts. We may have friends through Face book, LinkedIn or Whatsapp. The fact is, those friendship is not real.

When can people realise this?

In olden times, cash box of many might not be full, but their mind would always be rich. Now it is the opposite. Cash is plenty but the loving kindness is empty.

What is it due to?

Every one of us, barring no exception, wants success. But then what is success?

Is it amassing wealth, buying golden ornaments, possessing a palatial building, making frequent foreign trips, celebrating son's/daughter's luxurious marriage, getting degrees, being surrounded by people who flatter us?

Will all these only define success?

All the above questions were haunting my mind quite often.

While I am attempting to expose the darkness, I feel I should show some light for dispelling that darkness. Through this book, I am attempting to suggest workable solutions to the issues like the ones mentioned above. My humble opinion is that by balancing the six wheels of life-Physical, Mental, Family, Career, Social, Spiritual – one can achieve Bliss and Peace, which should be the ultimate objective for anybody. One without the other will not be of any use. All the six are interwoven. This book emphasizes that fact. ***It is my earnest wish that the word LIVE has to be spelt as pronounced in '*****LIVE** ***Programme'. By balancing properly all the Six Wheels of Life, one can '*****LIVE*****' with Bliss and Peace.***

How far I have travelled in that direction, is left to the decision of the readers.

With HIS grace and by the Divine Blessings of Mahaperiva, the Great Mahan,who is my guiding divine force,I could gain enormous experience in many corporates and get interaction with people of all walks of life. Not only that. Goddess Sharaswathi showered me with good collections of anecdotes and stories through many – both known and unknown. This book is the result of all the above. Nothing great for me. All Glory goes to God Almighty!

I will be the happiest person, if the reader has the following as the take-home message from this book:-

- *If you are financially rich, spare a portion to the needy*
- *If you are physically strong, do the needed physical assistance to the nearby society*
- *If you are knowledgeable, share that knowledge to the needy*
- *If you are an entrepreneur, provide jobs to the deserving*
- *If you are spiritually advanced, spread that light to the people around*
- *The ultimate luxury is being healthy, being happy, leading a contented married life, having an affectionate family, being with loving friends, living in an unpolluted place*
- *The mark of a true human being is not in his knowledge but with his humility. Your intellect and education are of no use, if they feed only to your ego*

It is my humble wish (request as well), that everybody may set an example in the balancing of six wheels and spread that power to the surroundings. If that circle is enlarged, the area, the village, the district, the state, the country and ultimately the world, will be a nice place to live with Bliss and Peace in abundance. Then we can experience and enjoy the heaven even in this materialistic world.

I consider the above as the ultimate message to the society, through this book.

Let Mahaperiva be with us in all our endeavours.

M. Harihara Mahadevan

Kanchipuram

M-9841356075

To Derive the Maximum Benefits Out of this Book......

The title of this book, ***LIVE WITH BLISS AND PEACE*** is very closer to my heart. I have taken sincere efforts to collect updated information from various sources, so that the readers can derive maximum benefits in all facets of life – Personal, Career, Societal and Spiritual etc. Mere grasping of information furnished in this book is one part. I request the readers to go through the learning, take away, moral etc given under each module. But I recommend those concepts have to be chewed and digested properly for proper assimilation. Proper application of those concepts in all spheres of life by the reader will alone complete the process.

To make that process very practical, I have attempted to correlate the well known Traffic Signal Concept with the practical application of the learning from this book. For your easy reference, the same has been given hereunder:-

The above Traffic Signal Concept can be extrapolated for any assimilation process –be it through attending a training programme or by reading a book. That can be explained as follows:-

Red – Implies stop

Amber – Implies pause and change

Green – Implies continue what you are doing well already

I would request you to pause for a while after each and every module and have an honest reflection on your present state of things, in respect of the concepts dealt with in that specific module.

Are you in the category of red, amber or green? Please have a self introspection.

For your easy understanding, I have given the example of allotting one hour for taking care of your body (as given in Physical Wellness module of the book)

If you are sure that it is coming under Green – being done on a regular basis – please give a pat on your back. Please also ensure that it is done on a sustained basis .

If you think that it is not being followed and it comes under the category of Red, have a resolution that you should stop that negligence gradually in your practices. Please have a time line for doing so.

If you consider that it is being done not on a regular basis but occasionally, you have to pause for a while and try your best to change that habit for betterment. Here also please have a time line for doing so.

This approach has to be followed for all the relevant practices, to be made in all the modules given under various wellness practices.

Please document your responses on the space given at the end of each chapter.

All the best for deriving the maximum benefits through this book!

You can reach me for any clarification through my mobile cum Whatsapp number. I will be happy to assist you.

M. Harihara Mahadevan

9841356075

Balancing of Six Wheels...

In the final analysis, you set an example, in the balancing of six wheels and spread that power to the surroundings... Then you can experience and enjoy the heaven in your life.

Peace Amidst Turbulence

There was a king. He told his minister to announce the entire kingdom about a contest for the artists.

A picture had to be drawn, depicting the peace. The best entry would be rewarded. Ample number of entries were received. The minister shortlisted two from them.

The first was on a calm, serene lake with a clear sky above. Beautiful forest with greeneries around the lake. "'Very nice", joyful king applauded.

"What about the second?". Enquired the king." Here it is "showed the minister.

There was a roaring, fierce waterfall. Dark clouds were threatening to pour the torrential rain at any time.

'Where is the peace here?" the king rebuked the minister.

"Pl observe the picture patiently my lord" the minister replied politely and calmly.

'Do you observe a rock by the left side of the picture?"

"Yes"

'Do you see a small tree, sprouting from the crevice of the rock?'

"yes" said the king. "You need not explain the rest. I got it. A mother bird was feeding its children in a nest on a branch of that tree. Ah! Excellent! Select this. What about your choice?"

"Yes, my lord! My choice coincides with yours. Great people always think alike" said the clever minister.

The take away from this anecdote is:-

Peace is not something, which can only be achieved in a calm environment. Amidst all the trials, tribulations and the odds of our turbulent life, if we are able to reach is the real and ideal peace.

In each and every part of our life, we are flying with wings, to earn our livelihood, supporting our family. We have no time to stand and stare. We tend to think that, we will settle after a specific period of our life – but we end up in realising, that period has not yet come. That is the saddest tale of human life. Not only that. We are tempted by many evils.

Buy one, Get Others Free.

We are living in this competitive world, where we get a' FREE', if we buy a specific commodity. We are becoming a prey, to those marketing gimmicks. Unfortunately, we are unconsciously becoming the victims, to our own self imposed traps. What are those traps?

- ***We unnecessarily buy anger, resulting in buying unwanted acidity.***

- ***We buy jealousy, leading to undesired headache.***
- ***We get into hatred, the by product of which, is ulcer***
- ***We involve in excessive stressful activities, inviting Blood Pressure.***

Instances such as these are more in this mechanical world.

The three hidden enemies, behind all these negatives are:-

Worry! Curry! & Hurry!

Worry due to our mind, Curry due to our mouth and Hurry due to our actions. In that way, our own organs do considerable harm to us.

Is there any way out, to overcome these negatives? As only light dispels darkness, these negatives can only be dispelled by positives like:-

- ***Do exercise, which can buy health***
- ***Have trust, which can buy harmony in relationship***
- ***Develop love, which can buy good virtues***
- ***Practice honesty, which can buy good sleep***
- ***Carry out righteous things, which can buy divine blessings***

Please mind that, all these acts, are at no cost.

So, we have to remember,

Solution lies in us, not coming from outside: we are only responsible for our own health.

Health apart, many are not clear about Success.

Every one of us, barring no exception, wants success.

But then, what is Success?

Is it amassing wealth, buying golden ornaments, possessing a palatial building, making frequent foreign trips, celebrating son's/daughter's luxurious marriage, getting degrees, which form the tails behind our names, being surrounded by people who flatter us?

Will all these only, define success?

A big NO!

A complete soul satisfaction is only success.

What is that soul satisfaction? From where, can we get that satisfaction?

Before going into the answer,

Let us visit a road side restaurant:

A farmer, who used to get up early in the morning, would harvest all the fruits and vegetables, cultivated in his own garden. He would start by 7 AM to go to the market, nearer to his village. Normally all those fruits and vegetables, would be sold by 12 noon and he would long to have the lunch, served by his affectionate wife, at home. On that particular day, it took 2 PM, for the sales to be completed. He had no patience to go home for lunch, since his stomach gave warning signals. He was searching for a road side restaurant, spotted one and went inside hurriedly.

The conversation between the restaurant owner and the farmer went like this:-

"Do you have anything that will quench my hunger?"

"Yes, but only Vadas, since all the other items were sold out"

"Will it quench my hunger?"

"Surely"

The farmer was served with vadas… One, two, five… His hunger was not satiated even after the 6th vada. Seventh was served.

"Ah! Now I feel satisfied with my stomach."

"Very glad"

"Thanks, how much will I have to pay?"

"70 rupees"

"Seventy?"

"Yes sir! You had 7 vadas. Each costs Rs 10. So 70."

"That all fine, but what did I ask you, before you served vada?"

"Will this vada quench my hunger?"

"Correct, but, which vada quenched my hunger?"

"7th vada"

"So, I will pay only for the 7th Vada, since it only satiated my hunger"

The poor restaurant owner was speechless.

Let us not go into their pointless quarrel, but quickly come back to the reality.

Like the farmer, who wants his hunger satiated, every one of us wants Bliss and Peace in our life, which is the seventh vada. Just as the seventh vada alone cannot satiate the hunger: all the previous vadas consumed, are all also responsible for the task, this Bliss and Peace, cannot come all on a sudden. There are six factors, responsible for that.

Those six are:-

Physical wellness

Mental wellness

Family wellness

Career wellness

Social wellness

Spiritual wellness

All these six wellness, are responsible for attaining Bliss and Peace in one's own life. It is not enough if one fulfilled a few, neglecting the others. One without the other will not serve the purpose.

The take away, from this vada episode in the restaurant is:-

We have to balance these six wheels of life. Perfect balance in each, by allotting time for all the six, will lead to a Blissful and Peaceful Life.

It should, therefore, not to be construed, that we have to apportion equal time for all these six. It is to be remembered that, ***depending on one's career, possible time for the other five has to be allotted.***

A social worker, who spends more time for his service, but if he neglects his family, it would not be of any use.

A person who cares only his family, without any help to the society, will not have satisfaction.

The catch to be made here is:

- ***If you are financially rich, spare a portion to the needy***
- ***If you are physically strong, do the needed physical assistance to the nearby society***
- ***If you are knowledgeable, share that knowledge to the needy***
- ***If you are an entrepreneur, provide jobs to the deserving***
- ***If you are spiritually advanced, spread that light to the people around***

So on and so forth……

In the final analysis, you set an example in the balancing of six wheels and spread that power to the surroundings. If that circle is enlarged, the area, the village, the district, the state, the country and finally the world will be a nice place, to live, with Bliss and Peace in abundance. Then we can experience and enjoy the heaven in our life.

There is a term called Health Iceberg. It describes about those things, we focus on diet and exercises, which will give physical health. It also describes those that are ignored by us, viz Emotional, Environmental, Occupational, Mental, Social & Spiritual health. Unless we give importance to all these, our life cannot be a balanced one.

This can also be simply illustrated, by the following:-

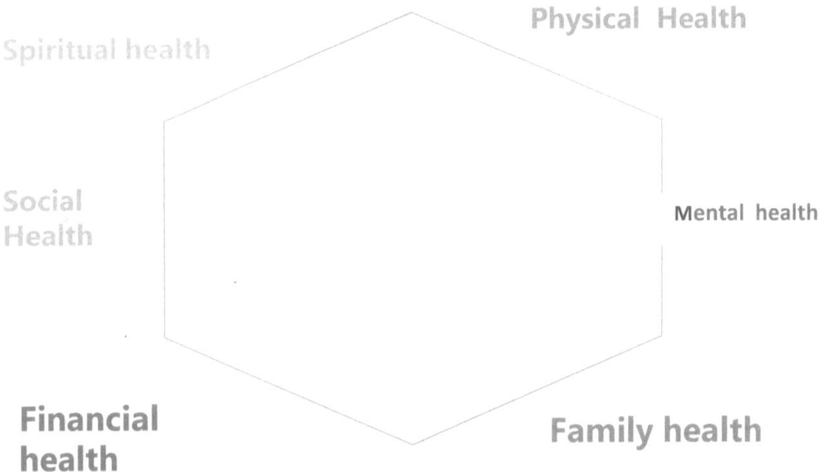

In the subsequent sections, we will deal with all the above six, one by one.

Reflections:-

Reflections:-

Physical Wellness

These are the very precious spare parts, created by God and it will be very difficult to replace them.

Acid Test

The acid test for one's wellness is – if one gets up in the morning without physical constipation and goes to bed at night, without mental constipation, he is said to have the wellness. If he is free from both physical and mental constipation, he will be a blessed person.

Let us see three known examples – all negatives:-

A friend of mine with three Ph.D in Chemistry – we used to say that his whole blood cells would be filled with chemistry. Alas! He spoiled his liver by his addiction to liquor. The entire first floor of his house would be like a bar, full of foreign liquor. He developed liver cancer, died at the age of 52, without carrying out his responsibilities as a father. It was true, that he did produce many Ph.D, but he failed to do his duty as a father to his two loving daughters and as a husband to his beloved wife.

A very famous person in Chennai produced many IAS , through his coaching institute, but he could not withstand the mental agony, due to the reasons known to him only. As a result, he committed suicide.

A prominent grocery merchant with amazing wealth, without an iota of care for his health. At the age of 45, he suddenly collapsed due to cardiac arrest.

All these three cases reveal that these people at the crucial period of their life and at the age, when their families look in for them, suddenly left the world, due to the sheer neglect of their health. Whatever might be the wealth or fame, they earned, were of no use, since they did not care to bother about their well being.

All of us are interested, to build a beautiful house to live in. We will do meticulous planning for the selection of the required materials and necessary things to decorate it. But the million dollar question is,

How many of us are able to live happily forever in that beautiful house built by us, with utmost care and meticulous plan?

The answer will be a miserable NO.

The house can be compared to the beautiful body and mind given to us by God. We fail to take care of the body and mind, resulting in loss of precious health and ultimately the life.

As seen earlier, the three things, which are the worst enemies, for our health are:-

Curry

Hurry

Worry

First Comes the Curry

The food we consume will tell a lot about our health. If we ask the question who is our life partner, answer will come immediately as the spouse.

But it is not the correct answer. Our life partner is very obviously, our body. It will tell us, which food or stuff or which activities are good for us. We should scrupulously obey its request. If it says, please don't take this food, or this quantity will suffice, we should not discard its request. It cannot speak, but that ***"body language"*** will be revealed by the ailments that follow, after its request is declined.

The stomach knows the nature and the limit of the food stuff that suits it. We should obey that warning signal. Or else we will be the worst sufferers. Same applies to our physical exercises and activities. All human beings are not alike. Each body is unique and it has its strength and limitations. One should do only those exercises, that suit one's body and should not be overdone.

We should not ignore the warning signals sent periodically by the different organs of our body. Eye will get scared, by the continuous use of electronic gadgets, Kidney is afraid of waking at night, cold food will make the stomach scared, smoking will frighten lungs, liver is afraid of fatty food, heart by salty food, pancreas by excessive sweets, intestines by overdose of non vegetarian stuff.

These are the very precious spare parts created by God and it will be very difficult to replace them. So let us make these organs happier, in turn they will provide happier life for us.

It has been proved, by scientific research that we can speak to the different parts of our body. Those organs can listen to our conversation. When we do a particular exercise or yoga, it will be better, if we tell the concerned part, that we are doing that particular exercise, to its benefit. Same way, if we take a specific medicine for a particular ailment of an organ, we need to tell that this medicine is consumed for curing that ailment. The cure, in that case, will be faster. Hindus will pray to Lord Muruga, with a prayer called, Skantha Shashti Kavasam, wherein, they will mention each and every part invoking God, to protect them. It is believed that, if we visualise that part, while reciting, the effect will be multi fold. Same way, there is a Meditation called 'Self Healing ' by Grand Master Choa Kok Sui, in Pranic Healing Practices, where in the practitioners will be asked to visualise different organs of the body to be healed, as the Master, conducts that guided Meditation. All of course depends upon one's own faith.

God also has given many foods that will help to maintain a good physique. Rujuta Diwekar,_author of the well known book, ***Indian***

Super Foods and a renowned Dietician, recommends the following food items for a healthier body:-

Rice, ghee, coconut, ground nut, cashew and jaggery which are all grown in India are good for our stomach. She also advises that millets are to be taken in moderate quantities. She also says that dinner should be finished two hours prior to sleep. To the question, how much of food stuff, one should take, she answers **please follow your stomach's advice.** She also recommends 150 minutes exercise per week and good sleep 6–7 hours per day There is no substitute for walking. Avoid tension at all times. Scrupulous following of her advice will make us maintain good health, and our life partner will be happy to cooperate with us.

Next Comes the Worry

Worrying cannot solve our problems. Rather it will only aggravate. There is no lock manufactured, without a right key. Same way, a problem will not be given by God, without a proper solution. We should always form part of a solution, not of the problem itself. If a problem erupts, think calmly and solution will surely come. One cannot see his face in a turbid water. Same way, we cannot find solution to a problem, with an agitated mind. Worrying will affect our heart and the whole body. Certain problems cannot have solution. Just accept that harsh fact and reconcile to the harsh reality.

The Last Comes the Hurry

As the old adage goes, ***Haste makes waste***. Any job done, without any forethought, will invite trouble. Hurried people will be stressful and their efforts will not bring the desired results. The hormone adrenaline will be secreted erratically, the stress hormone cartisol will shoot up the blood pressure and the person will be subjected to multiple diseases.

Whatever said and done due to our negligence, we are subjected to many hardships in our life. There exists a curse for many. What is that curse?

Every human being will have three phases of life:-

First phase, where they will depend upon their parents, for money, as some body points it out they adopt POM-playing on other's money. They will have ample energy and more time at their disposal. They will have more time and energy but less money. **Second phase**. They get an employment, when they will possess enough money, sufficient energy as well, but they will say (rather they will have a fashion to say) that they don't have enough time at their disposal. **Third phase.** Well, they move on to the old age, when they would have earned a sizable amount, still more time at their disposal, but the energy level would have started deteriorating. They will have a late realisation now, that they have not taken care of their health. They ought to have taken more efforts, at their early stage itself. This is the human curse.

Many of us tend to earn more money. If we try to spend some time, to earn good health, it would have been better. **Old age is a bank account** – whatever we save in our early life – wealth and health account, those alone will come back in that stage of our old age

The bottom line is – we should spend the required time for our health, starting from our young age, continue till the old age. Many fail to do that, like the rich person mentioned hereunder:-

There was a rich business magnet, celebrating his daughter's marriage, in a very extravagant manner, with delicious food varieties, with 6 assorted sweets. While the lunch was being served, he was looking here and there and suddenly sat before a banana leaf. The contractor was happily serving, all the varieties to his master. When he was about to take a piece of sweet and try to taste, a lady's hand seized that sweet. There was a 'slip between the cup and the lip'. It was his wife, preventing her diabetes husband, from eating a sweet. While he was celebrating the marriage with all sweets, served to others, he could not enjoy them. That was his fate. He did not have the Bogam. Bogam is one of the sixteen fortunes, mentioned in our Tamil literature. It is the fortune in one's own life, where he will enjoy all, he had earned. This person was an exception for that bogam, since he was not bothered to take care of his health in his early age.

If one does any job with Ishtam (willingness), there will not be any kashtam (difficulty). If he does with kashtam, it will not have any ishtam. The rich person, mentioned above, probably might not have followed, the health practices with ishtam.

The thumb rule is, if you take care of your body for one hour per day, it will take care of you, for the entire 24 hours of your day.

The irony is that most of us, will have the laziness, started right at our getting up in the morning. We may get up physically, but our mind will prevent us to do so.

The crux of the point emphasized here is, that physical wellness is the first and foremost practice in one's own life and for that, the body, or the life partner, has to be well taken care of.

In that connection, it will be worthwhile to realise the wonderful benefits of walking, which will be the major contributor for our physical wellness.

It is pertinent to know that, we have everything as medicine in Indian System of cooking. Food is the medicine. Kitchen is the clinic, if you follow that food system. In that system,

Health Tips

The six essentials, one should not miss in daily food items, are:-

6 Essentials

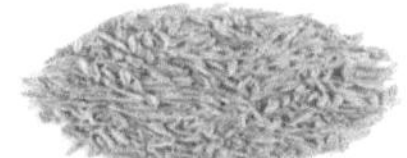

Instead, today's younger generations consume the opposite, which spoil their health. Packed and packaged foods are the most wanted ones in today's world, which erode one's health Liver is the most important organ of our body, which carries out more than 500 functions. These kinds of artificial, fast and junk food, will affect our liver in due course, which eventually will lead to death. Even a peck of liquor per month, will be enough to affect the liver in the long run.

Latest Japanese research has proved that many diseases are psychological in nature and are caused by our own negative tendencies.

WORRY, CURRY, HURRY are the major causes of many ailments.

Worry comes, because of our Tamas Guna (as described in Bhagavat Gita) and it releases the stress chemical called Cortisol, which will result in stress and high blood pressure.

Curry arises out of – Tamas Guna, resulting in acidity causing stomach ailments.

Hurry is because of Rajo Guna, that releases excessive adrenalin leading to stress.

Acidity is not because of what we eat, but that eats us. It is caused by our negative mental attitude.

Hypertension is not only due to salt, but with negative attitude.

Cholesterol is not due to fat, but due to the present day life style.

Asthma is not due to breathing problems, but due to miserable state of mind.

Diabetics is not due to sweets intake, but due to the stubborn attitude.

Kidney stones are not due to calcium oxalate, but due to suppressed emotions and hatred in heart.

Spondylitis is not only L4 L5 or cervical disorder, all due to excessive stress or unnecessary anxiety about future

If we are able to overcome these negative feelings, we can guard against the above diseases.

About Diabetes and BP

If our own food eats us, it is diabetes. If it is digested properly, it is health. If one's own thoughts block one's heart, it is BP. It is because, we are obsessed continuously, with a particular thing or a problem, it turns into BP and spoils one's health. Without attending to the root cause of the problem, if we take tablets for BP, we will end nowhere. Without taking tablets, if we set right the problems in us, we can come back to normal healthy life. If we continuously take tablets, we will reduce the functioning of heart. **That is called lock down for the heart**

Same way if we eat after hunger, our food becomes the much needed energy. If we have mechanical eating habits, and with eating tablets for diabetics, **we produce a lock down for our digestive system**. The point we have to remember is, we should know the body and its organs' functions and our actions should be in synchronous. with that. We get proper immunity from diseases-be it BP or diabetics.

***Are we going to produce lock downs to our system or to gain immunity? The choice is* ours.**

Ancient Systems of Food

The ancient system of foods, (which they call as Arusuvai in Tamil) followed in south India, gives prominence for six tastes. They are:-

1. Astringent, which will stimulate the formation of blood cells. This is abundant in Raw banana, fig, pomegranate, turmeric etc
2. Sweet, which is important for healthy tissues. This is abundant in rice, wheat, carrot, fruits etc
3. Sour, which provides fat. This is abundant in curd, tomato, tamarind etc
4. Pungent, which aids in the growth of bones. This is abundant in ginger, onion, garlic, pepper etc

5. Bitter, which strengthen the nervous system. This is abundant in bitter guard, til, fenu greek etc
6. Salty, which aids in secretion of saliva. This is abundant in raddish, pumpkin, greens etc

Regular intake of these types of foods in diet, will enable one, to get a balanced diet, which will help, in maintaining good health. Old is gold will apply to food intake too.

About the Vital Organ Liver

Many will skip their breakfast, which will be very bad for their health. There is a huge gap between dinner and breakfast. We have to break that fast. That is why, it is called breakfast. Many commit another big mistake of having late dinner, which will affect their liver, the most precious and costly organ of human body. *We cannot imagine, how much trouble and torture, the liver is undergoing to digest the food, taken very late,* that too, a non vegetarian food or maida. If we take an abdomen scan after a late dinner, we can practically observe that. Let us finish the dinner at least by 8pm. If we are taking late dinner, let us stop with only milk and biscuit. It may result in acidity, but with a heavy dinner, it may lead to serious consequences as warned by Gastro specialists. If we chew the food thoroughly, it will be digested properly and chances of getting diabetics are less. *Moreover, use of rice cooker in our kitchen, will increase the carbohydrates and it may lead to diabetics.* This has been found out in recent studies

Adequate Sleep

Another important aspect of maintaining health depends on sufficient sleep, say 6–7 hours of sleep. Deprived of sleep will affect the functioning of pancreas, which along with the cortisol level (to make us awake) will result in the higher glucose level in the blood stream. Moreover, there will be a tendency to eat, which will also increase the glucose level. We should never go against the restorative stage, during the sleeping cycle of body. Let us sleep well and maintain a good health There are certain mudhras and yoga which will help the digestion.

Fasting

We should do intermittent, periodical fasting, which, it has been found out, will even kill cancer cells. Our ancestors have advised for fasting-Hindus for Ekadasi, Muslims for Ramalan and Christians for Easter. Recent Japanese Research, has coined a term called **Autophagy, which denotes cellular housekeeping, by which damaged cells, pathogens are degraded and removed from cells. This house keeping will be hastened by fasting. Health experts advise for 12 hrs fasting, once in a week or at least in a fortnight, wherein, we can finish the dinner before 7pm on a day, have the beverages only by 7am on the next day. This 12 hrs fasting, periodically, will take care of our vital organs and ultimately our health**

There is one aerobic exercise called Nitric Oxide Blow out, which will strengthen the heart and will reduce the blood pressure.

One Leads to Other

Our physical and mental health are interrelated. One affects the other. A healthy diet will lead to a well maintained body and in turn to a healthier mind. A calm and peaceful mind will lead to a healthier body.

I recall an anecdote during the II world war. The prisoners were subjected to various tortures. One such was with a cobra bite. A researcher started doing a study with this. He chose two prisoners for his study. One was as usual subjected to cobra bite. He died. Another prisoner was made, to observe his fellow prisoner, meeting his death with cobra bite. A live cobra was shown, moving towards him. Then the second one was blind folded. He was not given cobra bite, but only a piercing with a needle. To the surprise of the researcher, the second one died after a while. Upon analysis of his blood sample, it was found to have the cobra poison. He concluded that his body system itself produced the cobra poison that killed him. Fear killed him more than the poison. Our mind can make or mar anything. The thoughts are very powerful and one should take care of it carefully. More than the medicines-be it allopathic or ayurvedic, if we don't believe its efficacy, it won't work out, to cure the disease.

Bane or Boon?

Diseases are not bane. Let us consider them as a boon. They are the warning signals reminding us that, we have not taken care of our health properly. Be precautious about the impending diseases.

If they affect us, do all the steps to overcome. Please don't get frustrated with those ailments. Every human being is susceptible to ailments. Nobody is an exception

You *should know that, there are varieties of medicines which are not available in medical shops. They are:-*

- Optimum exercise
- Walking
- Periodical fasting.
- Eating & merry time with family
- Laughter
- Sound sleep
- Mingling with people
- Determined to be happy
- Thinking positive
- Wishing & blessing others
- Keeping silent
- Loving kindness
- Calm and composed mind

You should be happy to know that, these are absolutely free and can be got in one place. It is in you and in your own self.

Hints on Good Health for Senior Citizens:-

One to Six

One

You are the Key person

Two things – for monthly check up:-

- BP and Sugar

Three white poisons – S, to reduce to the minimum on your foods:-

- Salt
- Sugar
- Starchy products

Three things – you need to forget:-

- Age
- Past
- Others' mistakes

Four things – to increase in your foods:-

- Greens/Vegetables
- Beans
- Fruits
- Nuts/Protein

Four imperative things – no matter, if you are weak or strong:-

- Friends who truly love you
- Caring family

- Positive thoughts
- A warm home

Five things – you need to do to stay healthy:-

- Fasting
- Smiling/Laughing
- Exercise
- Reduce your weight
- Voluntary work

Six things – you have to follow:

- wait till you are hungry to eat
- wait till you are thirsty to drink
- wait till you are sleepy to sleep

But please don't wait:-

- Till you feel tired to rest
- Till you get sick to go for medical check-ups (otherwise you will only regret later in life)
- Till you have problem, before you pray to your God.

Golden Advice from a doctor for Senior Citizens:-

- *Make a habit of practising silence for a few minutes, immediately after rising from bed*
- *Have an attitude of gratitude for life*
- Don't fall down *is the thumb rule for elderly people. Since, falling paves way for the beginning of ending.*
- *Keep walking. Walking is living. Those who can't walk, due to medical reasons should try pranayamam or breathing exercises*
- *Keep hydrated, since they are prone to dehydration. Drinking water by sipping frequently, butter milk, coconut water, etc.*

- *Good bowel and gut health. Eat fiber rich foods*
- *Be active mentally and remain cool*
- *Be cautious about Alzheimer's and Parkinson diseases and depression.*
- *Keep the brain active by the activities, that are of interest*
- *Have the habit of reading. Writing and reading will engage the old*

Let the advice/tips mentioned be followed by all for a sound physical wellness

Reflections:-

Reflections:-

Mental Wellness

The acid test for one's own wellness is, if he gets up early in the morning, without physical constipation (mala chikkal as we call in Tamil) and if he goes to bed, without any mental constipation (mana chikkal as we call in Tamil). Rest is assured, that he has got good wellness.

Mind Your Thoughts

> ***When HE closes one door, it is HIS intention, to open some other doors.***

Thoughts play a very prominent role. If one minds his thoughts properly, he can lead to a peaceful life. But, then, is it possible? What all will come into play?

Let us go into a classic piece of Ki. Rajanarayanan, a famous writer in Tamil. In his piece called ***Karisal kaattu kaduthaasi*** (a letter from a barren land) he mentioned about a farmer, whose routine was to go to his farm, with the pudding prepared by his loving wife, to finish all his farm work and to return in the evening. On one such day, while he was having his pudding, it appeared to him, that a tiny chameleon had fallen into his pudding and he had swallowed that. With that impressions and feelings haunting him, he stopped his work and returned home. With very much anguish in his mind, he narrated to his wife all the happenings. His wife set aside his worries and said all were only his imaginations and nothing else. He was not convinced. He did not have his food and sleep. He said to his wife that he had swallowed that chameleon. It was creating much problem in his stomach and he would die soon. He became very weak. His wife started worrying. Took him to his family doctor. The doctor patiently heard, all she had narrated. He checked his pulse and his body thoroughly. He thought for a while and told that it was true that he had swallowed the creature. Unless it was removed from his body, he could not survive. He asked him to come on the next day, just before sunset. A herbal mixture would be given to him and that would flush out everything from his stomach, including the creature, inside his stomach.

All was done, as per his direction, on the next day evening. The doctor got a torch light and showed a dead chameleon in that vomited fluid. On seeing that, the farmer got much relieved and he thanked the doctor. Poor farmer did not know that the doctor treated him psychologically, making him believe that he had swallowed a chameleon, by placing a dead tiny chameleon beforehand in that pot, in which he vomited. He purposely asked him to come only at sun set, so that he could not notice that in the pot, prior to his vomiting.

The thought, that he had swallowed the creature, was deeply embedded in his mind. Unless it was erased from his mind, no medicines could work. The thought was so powerful, that made him mentally weak. Such would be the significance of thoughts.

The thought process can totally change the course of one's own life. Look at this fictitious story. An alchemist, who could not succeed 100% in his mission of conversion of iron into gold, was advised by a friend, if he reached at the top of Himalayas at a specific place, he could get the exact formula. The friend also cautioned him that he should restrict his doubt to only one question, since the person would not be there to answer further queries. The alchemist carefully listened to his advice and reached the designated place. The door was opened from inside. To the surprise of the alchemist, the person was a beautiful lady. The question that came from the mouth of the alchemist at that moment was," ***Are you married***?" 'No" the lady went inside, closing not only the physical door but also the path, for getting the required formula. It would be anybody's guess, on the outcome of the alchemist's research. The thought that came to his mind, at that spur of the moment changed his whole fate.

Many of us would have faced these kinds of situations, when our thought, at a specific moment, did abruptly change our life journey. The take away from this episode, is also that one should ask the right type of questions in order to get the right answer. But many ask the wrong questions, but search for the right answer. Which category do you belong to?

Power of Thoughts

Masaru Emoto

Courtesy:- Research by Masaru Emoto on thoughts

An interesting study, carried out by a Japanese researcher called Masaru Emoto, was on the power of thoughts. He took the same source of water in different bottles of same size and same material… He poured the water in those bottles and sealed it. He pasted different labels, at the outer part of those bottles, the wordings of which could be seen in the above pictures. He put those bottles in a refrigerator. The crystals formed out of those, were subjected to crystallography and the shapes got were also depicted in the above picture. Those bottles, with the labels bearing positive wordings, appeared very pleasant and soothing. Whereas those with negative wordings, appeared very frightening and fearful. He concluded that, when a small label could make these kinds of positive and negative impact, what about our thoughts, on our bodily system? Our body contains 70% water. Whatever thoughts or feelings we have, will have a greater bearing on our blood and it will affect us heavily. That was his conclusion, which is a scientific proof of the effect of thoughts on our well being.

Anxiety Turned into Worries

Another aspect of minding one thought, lies in our worries.

Anxiety is needed for better performance, but when it leads to worries, it will lead to adverse effects. Worries and the stone locked in a shoe, are the same. Unless they are thrown away, one can never rest in peace.

By worried thoughts, we can't achieve anything, they will spoil our mood, time and ultimately our health. If we can't come out of a worst situation, will the worries in any way, help us to overcome the situation?

When the mind is weak, situation is a problem, when it is balanced, it becomes a challenge, when it is strong, it becomes an opportunity. It is all our perception to the situation, that makes a difference. But are we like that? **Read the following story:-**

Some miscreants developed a crazy idea. They got hold of three goats, from the neighborhood and painted the numbers as 1, 2 and 4 on the goats. That night, they let down the goats inside a school premises.

Next day morning, the school peon smelled dirty inside the school. To his shock, he spotted the shit of the goats inside, and the whole school started searching for the goats. They could find out three goats with only the numbers 1, 2, 4. They were in search of the 3 and could not trace it out. Holiday was declared for the school and the entire school was involved in the search and they could not trace the number 3. The reason? It did not exist.

This analogy reminds us of the feeling, that we incur for the missing, nonexistent 'third' goat, even though we have everything other than the third goat. Whatever may be the area of complaint – be it in family, health, profession, finance, fame – the thing that emerges as common is, longing for something, that is absent, worrying for it discarding the presence of many other things.

The lesson to be learnt is, instead of worrying about the 'third goat', let us all cherish whatever we possess now. If there are no worries, life would be much pleasant. Let us not let that' third goat', into our mind and make our life miserable. Whatever given by God, let us be thankful to HIM and enjoy that, without worrying for the 'perceived missing.' Attitude of Gratitude is what is needed for a peaceful life.

On a Similar note Another Anecdote:

God appeared before some people. HE told them whatever they want, they could ask and it would be granted. Each asked whatever they wish to have. The first person asked for owning a big business and amassing wealth. The second one wanted to occupy a big position. Third person a lady, wanted to be the most beautiful in the world. Fourth one wanted to become the most famous actor. Like that all expressed their wish. God granted them, without any hesitation. The last person, the tenth one, asked HIM to give him, the best possible state of peace and happiness. All the others turned towards him and ridiculed him – we all asked GOD whatever we wanted, just to get these peace and happiness. If we got those, there would be no doubt that we would be peaceful and happier. God was listening to those words and told them calmly that they could leave, since they were granted, whatever they asked for. HE also told the tenth person to remain, since HE wanted to speak to him personally. He was asked to wait for a while and GOD left the place. All the other nine persons did not leave the place. They were curious and anxious, to know what GOD would talk to the tenth person. It was true that they all got whatever they wanted. But they had the emptiness in their mind that the tenth person is going to get something which was not given to them by GOD. That made them restless and without peace of mind. They became jealous of the tenth person.

What about the tenth person? He got the complete satisfaction that GOD was going to talk to him personally. That thought itself, made him peaceful and happier.

Let us all decide, which person we want to be, are we going to be among the mass nine, or the distant ten?

Sometimes, what happens is that, these kinds of worries turn into despair. We become depressed We conveniently forget that, this depression can be made into a consolation. How?

By our conscious realization that:

Rain is brought only by Broken clouds

Broken soil alone allows the plants to grow

Broken crop only turns into a seed

Broken seed alone gives life to plants

These are the wonderful lessons taught by God.

HE makes these things broken purposely, to be made use of them wonderfully.

Let us console ourselves, when we become broken in heart, we should realize that HE has got some other intention to make use of us, for certain specific good purposes.

When HE closes one door, it is HIS intention to open some other doors.

There is a person called ***S. Ramakrishnan in Tamilnadu****, who wanted to become a successful engineer. He, fell down during hurdles test, in the navy selection interview and became totally paralyzed below neck. He was depressed initially. Then he consoled himself and* *started very humbly, an* ***NGO called Amar Seva Sangam****, which spread its wing fast and became known globally. His service brought him, the prestigious* ***Padma Sri Award****. If he were bothered about the closed door, he would have kept himself isolated. His services could not have been available to the handicapped, through his NGO, Amar Seva Sangam. God might have had this noble purpose in mind, when he met with that accident, All happens with a purpose. Poor people, we are ignorant of HIS intentions.*

Manage Your Thoughts

A person with a goal in his mind should focus only on that goal, setting aside all other happenings.

Having seen, that thoughts are very powerful, it is worthwhile to see, how we can manage those thoughts.

Each and every moment, we are confronted with so many stimulus, acting on us. The way, we tend to face those, determines our success or happiness or peace

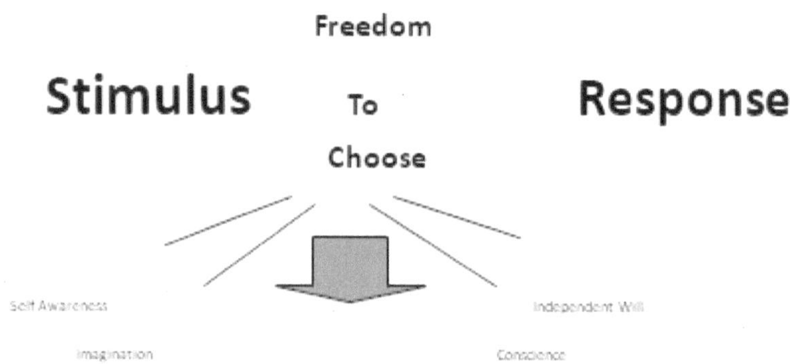

Source:- Stephen Covey's book on' The Seven Habits of Highly Effective People'

Between every stimulus and response, there is a thing called freewill or freedom to choose, which is given by God, to the human beings alone. Let us explain this concept with two examples.

Mother Theresa, who dedicated her life to service was in the process of collecting donation for an orphanage. The person approached by her, instead of giving money spit on her left hand. Without getting provoked or perturbed, she immediately asked him:

"You have given me spitting. What are you going to give for my children?" He stretched her right hand. That ashamed person donated money.

A similar incident. Madan Mohan Malavia, who founded Benares Hindu University, was approaching the Nizam of Hyderabad, for donation. Nizam got wild. How come this man approaching me for donation? He threw his right leg chappal upon Malavia. Malavia very gently took that chappal, went to the busiest street of the city and started auctioning that chappal. He told the surrounded people "this is the right leg chapal of Nizam. The auction proceeds will be used for the university". The news reached Nizam. He ordered his people to take part in the bid, so that it is given the maximum bid. The rest was history. Malavia got a huge amount in that auction.

The point to be noted in these episodes is, in between the stimulus, spitting, and her immediate response, Mother Teresa used her free will, thought for a while about her purpose. That purpose of collecting donation was her priority. Humiliation failed to bother her. All the other things were not in her agenda. She fulfilled her mission. Same was the case with Malavia.

A person with a goal in his mind should focus only on that goal, setting aside all other happenings.

What about many? They react immediately to the stimulus. If they give a pause, say a few seconds, they will respond, not react. Reaction will lead to undesired outcomes, whereas response will lead to favourable ones. A few seconds' pause will give one, the time for deep breath. resist the urge to act immediately, put the ego aside, think how to act, weighing the consequences. All these are the results of the free will, which we human beings, are alone bestowed with.

A Saint was doing meditation in an empty boat, on a sea shore. Suddenly he heard the noise of a boat dashing against his boat. Getting annoyed, he opened his eyes and started shouting "who dared to disturb my meditation?"

He could not notice anybody in that boat. It became clear to him that an empty boat came along the river by the natural flow of that water. He got ashamed. "I pose myself as a Saint. But I did have neither the concentration nor the patience. How this lifeless boat can have the motive of disturbing my meditation.? It was I who was disturbed in my mind." he felt ashamed of his act.

Many are like this Saint. If we don't have a proper sleep at a specific night, and if we hear the barking of dogs, we immediately jump into conclusion, that it is the dogs that disturbed our sleep. We are disturbed and not the dogs that disturbed our sleep. If our free will comes to our rescue at the right time, we will be calm and composed, irrespective of the external situation, however disturbing it may be.

We can also say that, ***this free will is the ability to control the quality and quantity of our 'internal dialogue'***

In his excellent book, ***Still Power***, Sports Psychologist Garret Kramer says that, a key factor to performing well in sports (and in life), is your ability to control the quality and quantity of your "internal dialogue". It can be given as an equation,

Performance = Potential minus Internal Interferences

However potential we may possess, if we are disturbed by internal interferences, our performance will be affected. Internal interferences are caused by the five sense organs, i.e. gyanendriyas as they are called in Hindu scriptures,

Influencing of Internal Dialogues

It means, how well we use our 5 gyanendriyas all the time, as it influences our inner dialogue. Here we have 100% free will

Avadootha Gita:-

In the famous piece of Hindu Scripture, Bhagavatha, a Saint Avadootha mentions about 26 Gurus, from whom he learnt lessons. Of these, the following five lessons, in respect of the five senses are to be mentioned specially.

He learnt a lesson form a male elephant, which was trapped by a hunter, through its lust with the female elephant. The sense **organ,**

body, breeds months of pain through the momentary pleasure. How many kingdoms and how many great people have fallen victims to this sensual pleasure? History tells many such stories.

There is a saying 'a fish dies by an open mouth'. A fish gets trapped by the fisherman, with his bait containing a worm. The fish, by his attraction towards the worm, is easily caught by the fisherman. Open mouth – either in terms of food or words – invites trouble. The Saint said he learnt lessons from a fish that he should be **careful with his mouth.**

A fly is attracted by the colourful light. It ends its life with that. Eyes are responsible for being victims towards gorgeous things – human beings or other beings. So one should be careful with his eyes. That is the lesson Saint learnt from the sense **organ called eye.**

A honey bee is attracted through its sense organ nose. It gets attracted by the smell of the flowers and it gets trapped. The Saint said he learnt a lesson that he should be careful with this sense **organ, nose.**

A deer is being trapped by the hunter by the music. The sense **organ, ear** is the victim to the sound and through that the deer is nearing its end. The Saint said he should be careful with this sense organ

So, as directed by Avadootha, if we are careful with these five senses and are self constrained, we can guard ourselves, against the external circumstances, and our mental wellness will be maintained.

In God's creations, we are surrounded by both good and bad, and beneficial and harmful. It is we who have to decide, which one we should employ or adopt or use.

Good and Bad Admixed

A Saint was giving lecture to his disciples. One disciple asked the Saint' Guruji! Both good and bad have been created by God. Why we should we use only the good? Why not bad? "To this pertinent question, the Saint told him to wait till that dinner, during which he would get the answer. During dinner all the other disciples were served milk, excepting that particular one, who was served both cow milk and cow dung. He hesitantly asked the Saint why? He replied "both are given only by the cow. You can consume both. Why are you apprehensive about taking the cow dung?" He replied "it will be bad for our health if it is consumed". The Saint told him to use the same wisdom, in choosing the good and bad, created by God. It is our free will that should come to our rescue, to employ only the good

In spite of that, we are confronted by good and bad and we are sometimes succumbed to the latter. Why? The answer given by one learned, is that we have two wolves inside us – one good and the other bad. Whichever is fed by us, will take over. It is our thoughts that feed those wolves. So we should inculcate only good thoughts, which will make the good wolf dominate over the other.

The above concept can also be explained by the following anecdote:

Don't Let Loose the Donkey

An evil spirit came and released a donkey, which was tied to a tree. The donkey ran into the fields and destroyed the crop. It was killed by a farmer's wife, who in turn was shot dead by the owner of the donkey. The farmer on hearing this, got angry and killed the owner of the donkey. The wife of the donkey's owner asked his sons to burn the house of the farmer and the task was carried out by them. To much of their sadness, the farmer escaped and he shot all of them dead.

An observer asked the evil spirit what was the reason for the worst mishap? "The evil spirit gave the answer, that it was true that he released the donkey, but all the others were only responsible, since they all were provoked and overacted. All due to the release of the inner devil in them. It also said that it did the task of waking all up, by triggering the ego and converting into evil intent.

Every one of us has this inner devil in us, we should be careful about the external trigger by the demon. We, therefore should use our free will, stop for a while and think before reacting, responding, reporting, rebuking or revenging. Before all these R's, the R, **React** comes first; we should be vigilant and careful about this R and guard us, against the untoward.

We should never let the inner devil out.

Destiny Can be Designed

Mind, those little compromises that you do daily, due to the negative thoughts, are the ones that will bring our downfall.

Can we design our own destiny?

Yes, we can. That process starts with our own thoughts. How? Swami Sivananda, the renowned spiritual guru, explains that in a beautiful way, by citing from four Yugas

At the start of the cycle of yuga, that is, Sathya yuga, all human beings were good. In the next in cycle, that is, Thretha yoga, (Ramayana period) people from one part of the world were good and in another they were bad-example, Lord Rama from Ayodhya was good and Ravana in Sri Lanka was bad. In the next cycle of Yuga, that is, Dwapara Yuga (Mahabaratha period), people in the same family were good as well as bad-example, Pandavas and Kauravas. In the present Yuga called Kali yuga, the same human being behaves good at sometimes, bad at some other occasions. The same mind has love and kindness sometimes and has hatred and anger at some other times. Both good and bad are manifested in the mind. Whichever is fed, by the concerned person, that will dominate. This feed is given by the thought process. That thoughts are responsible for the good or bad, manifested in an individual.

This thought process is explained vividly through Energy system:

Energy flows where Attention Goes. Everything in our Universe is Energy. We human beings are also Energy. So it is very important, to learn how Energy flows from us and how it affects our lives. Look at the following examples:-

When you say, "I don't desire War" attention is focused on war. In that direction of attention, your Energy will flow. Law of Attraction will fit into your Energy and make it real. If you utter, I want Peace, you are giving your Energy to Peace and Law of Attraction will match your Energy with Peace and your life will be Peaceful. Hence the Universe, thus works on Vibrations.

In the same way change your statements:

Instead of saying "I don't desire to get failure", say "I desire to succeed"

Instead of saying "I don't want to be obese" say "I want to be slim"

Instead of saying "I don't want to have a stressed career" say "I want to have a mentally rewarding career"

Instead of saying "I don't want to cross swords with my husband" say "I want to have a smooth passage with my husband"

and so on........................

Our thoughts are very powerful, because energy is transmitted through our thoughts. So give utmost importance to your thoughts. If you think and speak about what you don't want, you will only attract what you don't want! But if you stop talking and thinking about what you don't want and change your words and only think and talk about what you want, then you will start attracting what you want, and the negative things will go away from your life

Let us practice from today, the following:-

- ***Let us stop thinking and talking about things, that we don't want.***
- ***Let us remove few words, from our dictionary like -***
- ***Depression/Hatred/Failure/Illness/Disease/War/Fights/Anxiety/Struggle/Debt/Enemies/Terrible/Accidents.***
- ***Changing our thought patterns will help us channelize our Energy*** and ***our Life will change accordingly.***

That thought process will give Bliss and Peace to our life.

Mufti Menk, a Muslim cleric and Grand Mufti of Zimbabwe, is identified as Salami. He makes everything clear, in the best & easy way to understand.

See these wonderful words:

7 people are killed by buffalos every year.

500 people are killed by lions every year.

800 people are killed by hippos every year.

5000 people are killed by spiders every year.

7000 people are killed by scorpios every year.

10000 people are killed by snakes every year.

But the tiny mosquitoes, kill 2.7 million people every year.

Small 'sins', are hardly noticed by many, are the most deadly to your spiritual life. These small sins emanate from our negative thoughts and are neglected by us. Eradicate the negative thoughts, before they become embedded in your mind. Remove them on a periodical basis. Gossiping and small lies, that come out of negative thoughts, are committed more frequently and are deadly. ***Mind, those little compromises that you do daily, due to the negative thoughts, are the ones that will bring our downfall.***

Two things are employed by positive minded people – smile and silence. Whereas silence can avert problems, smile can turn problems to our advantage. When ants face a mixture of salt and sugar, only sugar will be chosen by them. Likewise, people with positive attitude, select only the right people, to have a pleasant and peaceful life.

***So, then, how to get rid of the negative thoughts and inculcate the positive thoughts?* Follow these Navarathnas:-**

1. *Meditation makes us, to be with positive thoughts. It drives the fear, anxiety and lead to a calm and composed life.*

2. *Smile is the best medicine. Laugh as deep as possible. There is an exercise taught in Meditation classes, called Laughing Buddha*

exercise. If we practice that regularly, it will remove all the negative energies from our system.

3. *Be amidst the company of positive minded friends. They will focus your attention to positive attitude. Develop a positive mental attitude. Whatever happens, happens only for good*
4. *Don't find fault with you or others. That will never help anyway. Even if something committed wrong, have the positive thought as to, how it can be made alright.*
5. *Lend your helping hand to the needy. The result of that action will make your thoughts positive*
6. *Practice forgiveness and gratitude. They are the two divine ways of bringing peace and happiness to one. That will enhance your positive thoughts.*
7. *Read only the positive news in the newspaper and the whatsapp. When getting up, start with the positive thoughts. The first thought that comes out, will make the whole day, shaped only with that thought. Hence be careful with the first thought*
8. *Come out of the multiple whatsapp groups. Have a selected group, with positive messages*

   Have the practice of switching off the mobile and whatsapp on a specified day. Spend that day with family and friends with the same wavelength.
9. *Spend 10 minutes in solitude. That is the time you spend for yourself. That time is the time your soul talks to you freely. Have that practice regularly.*

Free Will and Karma

This free will can be correlated with Karmic Theory.

According to Hindu Scriptures, there are three types of Karma. Good and bad deeds, accumulated over many births are called Sanchitha Karma. This can be compared to the human anatomy in which a person is susceptible to the whole lot of deceases in his life time, the total ailments in his life. Prarabdha Karma is the Karma, which a person has to undergo in the present life. This can be compared to the ailment, a person undergoes at the present circumstances. Agamya Karma is the karma is the one, which is created by the present acts of a person. If he is careful about that, he can avoid it, being included in the Sanchitha Karma. This can be compared to the precautions; one is taking to combat the decease undergone at the present circumstances. The free will is exactly the Agamya Karma. If a person is not taking proper care about his health, it will lead to many more deceases. Same way if he is not using his free will, it will land him in undesired consequences.

The free will can also be correlated in terms of a student, undergoing a college education. If he studies well, there won't be any arrears, in that semester, in the same way, if one uses his free will. If not his arrears will increase which will amount to total accumulated arrears for his degree course, like the gradual addition of Sanchitha Karma.

Covey and Sivananda

What Covey told in 1980s, Swami mentioned long back. Thoughts are only responsible for whatever happens to us-good or bad.

There is a classic book called "The Seven Habits of Highly Effective People" by Stephen Covey.

He mentions about Response Ability – the ability to take response, which is in our hands only. This author correlates that to free will… This book came in 1980s. Long before, the entire gist of the whole book, was given by Swami Sivananda from India, in a single paragraph, which can be picturised as follows:-

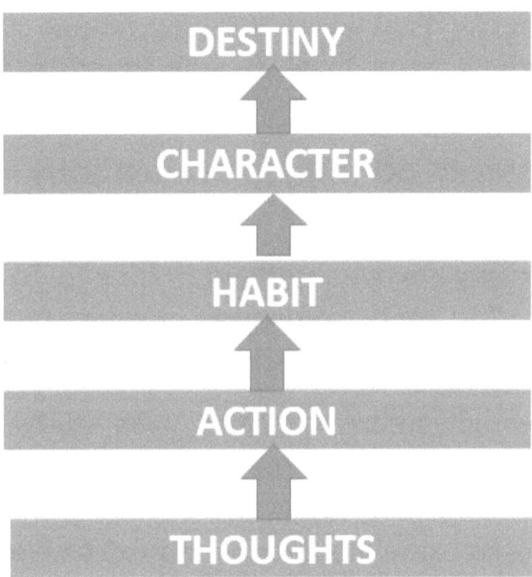

What Covey told in 1980s, was in perfect agreement, with what was told by Swami. Thoughts are only responsible for whatever happens to us-good or bad. If we are careful about the thoughts, then we can change the course of our life. We have to take up responsibility for that. That is what told by Covey through response-ability.

Get Rid Off Ego

Many carry ego unnecessarily in their head, making theirs and others' life miserable. Life journey will be smooth, if one passes that journey without ego.

Today's world is characterized by 'E 's, be it, e-commerce, e-mail e-ticket, e-governance etc. In English language, e is the most elite letter. E comes in men and woman. We cannot make a house without 'E'. Bread or Butter can't be found without 'E'. Existence starts with 'E' and ends with trouble. We won't find it in 'war' , but twice in 'peace'. Occurs once in hell but twice in heaven.

'Emotions' are not without 'E'. That is why, all relations, soaked with emotions, through Father, Mother, and Brother, Sister, Wife & friends have 'E" in them

Without 'E,' there are no love, life, wife, friends or hope. Finally no 'Life', 'Death' without 'E'.

Hence we should GO with "E" but definitely without a trace of E-GO

Even then, many are over burdened with ego. To teach them the proper lessons, God sends somebody or other. One such incident happened in the life of Swami Vivekananda.

When Naren (Swami Vivekanand) was studying law, at the University College, London, a professor, whose name say was X, disliked him intensely. One day, Mr X was having lunch at the dining room, when Naren came along and sat next to him. The professor said, "Mr. Naren, do you know that a pig and a bird do not sit together to eat?" Naren looked at him and calmly replied "You do not worry professor. This bird will fly away." Mr. X, terribly angered, decided to take revenge. The next day in the class, he posed the following question: "Mr. Naren, while crossing a street, if you noticed a package, and found two bags, one with wisdom and the other with money, what will be your choice?"

Without hesitating, Naren responded, "The one with the money, of course"

Mr X, with a sarcastic tone, said, "I will surely take the wisdom only"

Naren quickly responded, "Each one takes which is lacking in him"

Terribly angered professor, wrote in the answer sheet of the student 'idiot'and gave it to Naren Un perplexed Naren, thought for a while and returned a few minutes later and told "I could find only your signature Sir, pl give the marks"

The take away is, we should not mess with intellectuals with our ego. It will always boomerang.

It is not only teaching a fitting lesson to the egoistic persons. Sometimes humility will play a better role in teaching a lesson.

There was a great Poet in Tamil, called Kannadasan who wrote lyrics for Tamil cinemas. His specialty was, he would write the most difficult ideas in simple language, for the common man, to make him understand. At that time, one Tamil professor was giving a talk through All India Radio, piercing the poet, that he copied from Tamil literature and made into Tamil cinema songs Lot of listeners of that programme were giving compliments to her. It was a live broadcast. Suddenly one voice came in the air.

"Can I talk to you madam?"

"OK. What is your name?"

"My name is Kannadasan". The lady got shocked. Then Kannadasan explained very humbly to that professor:

"there were many many treasures from Tamil literature, about which, common man might not be aware of. I thought, the gist of that treasures should reach, even the remote corners of the state. That is why I took those pieces and simplified those to their understanding"

The lady felt sorry and sought an apology.

It was not necessary for that poet to come on line and explain his stand. But he did... That showed his humbleness. That is why his lyrics are still being talked about.

We should not be like the empty vessel that makes noise. Should be like a filled one, which remains silent. One of the greatest lessons taught in scriptures is Vinaya, the humility. It is a much needed quality in mental wellness.

In this hurly burly world, many are busy, in earning money, without bothering about their health and spending their free time, on modern electronic devices. They also indulge in undesired habits. It is better, if they try to replace certain harmful habits, embedded in them, into productive ones. That practice will definitely result in good physical and mental wellness. Those required replacements are listed below:

- ***Changing to Home – made Food from Fast Food***
- ***Proper Sleep instead of indulging in Whatsapp, Face Book*** **and** ***Netflix***
- ***Cultivating Fruitful Friendship rather than Spoiling Associations***
- ***Showing Gratitude instead of Groaning***
- ***Ownership replacing Blame Game***
- ***Productive Action instead of Obsession***

Reflections:-

Reflections:-

Family Wellness

Active listening involves two ears –one for the meaning and the other for the feeling of communication

Strike the Right Stroke

In this Family Wellness series, we are going to deal with relationship – be it in family or friend circle. Organisations give prominence to results, there relationship takes the backseat. Relationship is for results only. In family or friend circle, relationship is primary.

Another difference is in terms of strokes – both positive and negative and conditional and unconditional. In organisations, invariably conditional positive and negative strokes are employed (though there may be a very few exceptions) whereas relationship in family and friend circles, additionally unconditional positive and negative strokes are also employed. Stroke here, is the care and concern shown for the other person. Let us explain the concept of stroke with an experiment conducted by a psychologist with three monkeys.

The researcher took three younger monkeys, born out of the same mother and put them into three different cages in the same hall. All the three, were fed with necessary food and water at regular intervals. The only difference was in the following:-

The first monkey was given a pat on the back and the second one was pierced with a needle periodically. The third one was not approached at all (of course excepting during the occasions during which it was fed)

The above process was continued for six months. One monkey died after that period. It would be anybody's guess that the third monkey would be that one. The first one was recognised by the pat on the back. The second, by the negative act of being pierced by a needle. What about the third? It was not cared at all. That indifference was the cause for its death. An average healthy person can live without food but only with water for a month. He can exist for a week, without food and water. But can he live for a minute without air? No, that is the reason why it is called as praanavaayu or the fluid needed for one's life. It is physiological oxygen. The one that is also needed, for a living being, is psychological oxygen, which is called stroke. Without this stroke –either positive or negative, living beings cannot exist. That is the exact reason, the third monkey mentioned in the experiment above died.

A student went to his father for getting the signature for his progress report, which showed that he had failed in all the subjects. The father, without showing any reactions, simply signed the report… The son got perplexed. He expected at least a bang from his father. He expected that negative stroke.

A worker did a mistake in the shop floor. His supervisor, on noticing this without any word, simply passed by. He expected a rebuttal from him. That negative stroke was expected from him. Instances such as these can be multiplied

A mother was playing with her child. Realising that she had to cook the foods for the family she left the child, with a feeding bottle. Since the mother left him, the child was longing for his mother.

Knowing that she was not coming forth, he threw the feeding bottle and there was a cracking noise. The mother came and she gave a blow to the child. It longed, at least for that blow, which was a kind of stroke

Every one of us, is longing for this recognition. When it is given at the appropriate time, we feel happy, when it is positive or relieved at least, when it is negative. Where there is passive behaviour, we get agitated.

Listening

Don't we hear these oft – repeated statements in our day-to-day life?

"I should have been married to a pillar. That should have been better."

"I vented out my grievances to my manager. He was simply saying 'hum hum' without even looking at my face. I should not have gone to him, it was a sheer waste!"

"I was expressing my difficulties, for the completion of my assigned task. He never bothered to listen to my problems. Somehow it had to be done. My problems, were not at all a concern for him. I should have told all these to a wall. Probably it might have listened better."

"Finish your talk quickly! I have hell a lot of jobs to be finished. I don't have time to listen to your issues."

"Don't allow them to talk. Interrupt their conversation. If you listen to them, you will yield to them."

"I had vented my sad bosom empty. Whether the problem is solved or not, he had the patience to listen to my concern and grievances. That is a big relief for me."

The above statements reveal the importance of listening in a relationship, The problems in many organizations are the poor or absence of listening, on the part of the superiors when their subordinates approach them for airing their grievances. A recent HR study reveals that people don't leave organizations, but people-their immediate bosses. They are known for their poor listening.

The statements quoted above indicate the attitudinal problems like preoccupations prejudices casual attitude and egocentrism of the higher ups, that retard the listening process.

Significance of Listening

Communication is meeting of minds – as one of the definitions for communication goes, it should enable the relationship to be developed between the persons concerned. In that aspect, attitudinal problems should be sorted out, or otherwise, it will mar the relationship. Active listening plays a vital role, in sorting out many attitudinal problems. It removes the bias and creates a complete understanding between the concerned.

Listening with Two Ears

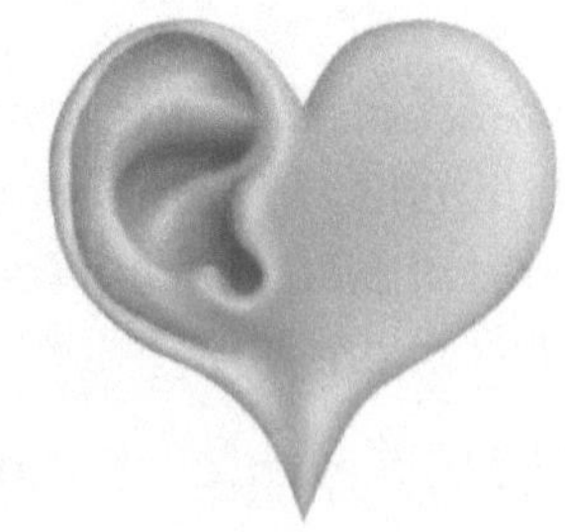

Active listening involves two ears –one for the meaning and the other for the feeling of the communication. During the end of the month May, a house wife tells her husband "See! The month June is coming". If the husband simply replies" yes! After May, June alone will come. What is new in that?" he is using his ear for meaning only. He does not understand the implied message – "that schools are reopening and you will have to arrange money for school fees, books etc for the children."

When an employee approaches his superior and tells him that his sister's marriage is taking place in another two months, the implicit message is that he wants leave and salary advance for the function. If the superior does not understand that message, he does not use the ear meant for feeling.

In many a situations, we come across-be it between husband and wife, son/daughter and the parent, worker and a supervisor, two close friends – if we pay heed to both the meaning as well as feeling of the communication, we have the active listening. In active listening we use not only the physical ear characterized by meaning but also the mind which is characterized by feeling of the communication. Many relationships get broken, because of this poor listening. Successful managers are active listeners, using both of these ears and they maintain a cordial relationship. These managers encourage the other person to express freely and fully. He puts the other at ease. He is alert to the cues and of the non verbal behavior of the other, to get the total picture.

Imagine the following incidents – a teen-aged daughter, disturbed by the ugly incident in the college, approaching her father, or the supervisor, harassed by a militant worker coming to the manager's cabin – the father or the manager, can guess the untoward, that has happened, by active listening to the cues, inferred from the body language of the approaching person. The emotional contents can then be responded well and the other person can be consoled and comforted well. In that way, the father or the manager or for that matter any responsible person, can sow the seeds of confidence and trust to the affected person and it will build a lasting relationship. In many a situations, absence of this active listening is creating a wall between the persons instead of building a bridge, for productive relationship. The life line for any relationship is proper communication, of which active listening plays a vital role. The productivity and quality of those relationships will no doubt enhance the organizational effectiveness-either in family or business organization.

Empathic Listening

Another aspect of active listening is empathic listening. While sympathy is feeling for others, empathy is feeling with others. Putting ourselves in others' toes, understanding their problems, seeing things from others' perspectives are all part of empathy. If one has empathic understanding, he will appreciate the problems, faced by the other person and his listening will be effective. He will appreciate the other person both intellectually and emotionally.

For working couples:- If they develop proper empathy, they will listen to each other's difficulties, feelings and emotions, then there will be proper understanding between them. Each will have a patient listening, towards other's problems and there will be less or no friction between them. Thus empathic listening, will act as lubricating oil in the friction of their issues and concerns. The husband will help his wife in cooking and the wife will help her husband in his official duties and the demarcation between" your job and my job" will go off and a "feeling of our job" will permeate in their daily chores. This meeting of their minds will pave pay for a friction-free and a very smooth relationship.

While that is the state of family organizations, in business organizations also the same conditions will prevail:

A union office bearer:- If he understands the financial difficulties of the management and the management has concern for the workers' grievances, it will lead to a harmonious relationship, proper understanding, developed through empathic listening.

A worker and supervisor:- A worker will not have any grudge towards the supervisor, when given the deadlines for the task, to be completed with optimum resources. On the contrary, the supervisor will be patient enough to understand the genuine difficulties and concerns of the worker and he will be lenient in the task completion.

A marketing representative:- He will have to put himself in his superior's shoes and appreciate his concerns in fulfilling the sale targets and will put all his efforts to help him in achieving the same. Similarly, if that representative is not able to fulfill the set targets due to factors beyond his control, his superior will not be very rigid in the targets.

The same arguments can be quoted for the empathic understanding between the production and design/marketing/maintenance departments and each will understand the genuine difficulties faced by the other. In that way there will be smooth understanding, that will lead to better productivity with harmonious and pleasant environment in the organizations.

If everybody follows this active listening, where is the room for misunderstanding and unwanted problems in relationship? **The world will then be a heaven to live in.**

Listening Saved a Life

There is one of the most influential books, titled, '**Man's Search for Meaning**', written by Psychiatrist Viktor E. Frankl. It is based on his own experience in Nazi Camp and the stories of his patients. He mentions in that book, about his experience with a lady, who was saved by him, from committing suicide, by his active listening to her problems. Problems with listening lead to innumerable issues – in personal or organizational relationship.

Whose Role?

This empathic listening was preached for couples by many learned. Once the renowned Spiritualist, Vedathri Maharishi was handling a session for couples. He was telling about three qualities to be possessed by couples, viz give and take, adjustability and patience.

One lady stood up and asked Maharishi, who should show this to the other – husband or wife. Everybody was waiting eagerly for the answer. The reply came was – the person who has the real love, towards

the other should. Instead of ego, the real love should prevail between the husband and the wife. There was a thunderous applause from the gathering.

For Couples

Love between a couple does not mean that they should not have any dissimilarities and differences: it is marked by the occasions, when they stand together, despite all these.

Real Love or Pseudo Love

In a packed hall, there was a contest, **Made for Each Other** for couples. The judge selected two, from the contestants. He told the audience that he had shortlisted two. One has got 90 out of 100 and the other 10. Who should be chosen, he asked the opinion of the audience. The audience said uniformly, the one with 90. He said that he had chosen the other. Why and how? For the audience queries, he replied that particular couple with all their differences in their tastes and preferences, were able to live together for forty years and they told the truth. They were awarded with a brand new car by the sponsor. The function came to an end. The couple with the car key came nearer the gifted car. The wife was arguing with the husband "How many times have I shouted at you about learning the car driving? See, now we have to search for a call driver". The husband was moving around the car with more joy and astonishment. The wife again shouted at him saying " come on! stop going around, your knee will be affected. You will come and trouble only me, saying Janu, please rub this pain palm, I have severe knee pain"

The hidden love between them masked in their visible fight, was brought to light. No wonder, this pair was chosen as the best couple.

Love between a couple does not mean that they should not have any dissimilarities and differences, it is marked by the occasions, when they stand together despite all these. It is the one, that makes them stand together for decades without decaying their intimacy, during the hours of need. It is not the bonding that is formed at the first sight and gets broken even within a month or year of their marriage.

Child is the Father of Man

A teen aged girl studying in a college, interviewed her father, regarding a project she was doing. She asked several questions. The interview went like this:

What is your name?

My name is K. Ramasubramanian

Is it the same before and now?

Yes!

How many friends for you in your college days and also at present?

It was less while studying, but more now because of my business life

How about your health and what you do to maintain that?

I perfectly maintain my health through yoga, walking and meditation. I spend circle in personal and business life. one hour daily for physical exercises and 30 minutes for meditation

Will you do anything, against your willingness?

Not at all. I go strictly with my preferences and choices

Thanks dad. Please listen to the audio, I had interviewed another person well known to you. The daughter continued.

What is your name?

My name is Sarala Ramasubramanian

Is it the same before and now?

No! I was Sarala Krishnan before my marriage

(The father interrupts now, Oh! Your mother!)

How many friends for you in your college days and also at present?

I had lot of friends in my college days. But my friends at present are only the wives of those men in your father's business circle.

How about your health and what you do to maintain that?

I was maintaining good health before marriage. I was a cricket player. I gave birth to you and your brother through c-section. I want to do exercises. But...........time? To look after the family and other household chores, take a lot of time. I hardly find time to do physical activities

Will you do anything that will be against your willingness?

I was a pure vegetarian before marriage. During my college days, I would not even sit with my friends bringing non vegetarian foods for lunch. Instead, your father being a non vegetarian, I had to cook the foods, against my liking, since your father relishes it.

The husband was taken aback. He had never thought about all these so far. His daughter made him realize his mistakes.

Many husbands are like this person. They are blind to their wives' likes and dislikes. On the other hand, the wives do not openly reveal their preferences and choices. That happens in many families. The sacrifices made by the wives are plenty. There may the other sides of the story. But, in Indian culture there are many Saralas. Proper disclosure by one to the other and perfect mutual feedback between them will weed out the differences. A perfect relationship requires proper communication to air the differences between the concerned and trying to bridge the gap between them without suppressing them. This is of paramount importance in any relationship

Mirror Image

While we are talking about disclosure and feedback, mention about a mirror has to be made... When we are looking at a mirror, it will give the exact picture of ourselves, no less nor more. It will give the status without getting emotional. It will give the status as we are in front of the mirror – neither exaggerated nor depreciated. While it is giving our exact picture, we don't get angry with it. We simply accept it. Moreover the mirror does not give any of our status, when we are away from it. It gives only face to face.

Mirror teaches us vividly about giving feedback. Honest feedback – without any prejudice, without any anger or other undesired emotions and without any backbiting – are all to be followed in any relationship. That will eradicate the misunderstanding and enhance the mutual relationship.

Anger and ego are to be totally avoided, in any family or other relationship. Anger is one word short of danger. Hence we have to be very cautious about it, since it will spoil the relationship.

While these are the general guidelines in any relationship of all ages, those specific to middle age, can be enumerated as follows:-

If we ask the husbands of the middle aged, about their conversation with their wives, the answer would be invariably on the negative side. Problems will be there in every family, in some form or other. If the couple are below 30, a mere physical relationship will set right the issues. If they are above 50, a mere touch or sight will turn the issue to the other side. If the couples are in between 30 and 50, there will be a huge gap between them. The communication would be very minimal. Most of the conversations would have been centred around family problems – like school issues, religious expenses, housing and vehicle loans. With all these, they will always be in stressed mind set and amicable and loveable conversations will be very rare.

When they reach 50s and they introspect about their past, they realise their past mistakes and they will be facing the criticisms from their daughter in law. "What have we achieved in the past, when we were struggling to uplift our families?" – these types of questions will definitely come up in their mind.

Better Late than Never

They have to think of the past and their moral obligation to their wives – appreciate their wives, help them in kitchen, family chores, take them out once in a month. Family communication is very important and the husbands should never overlook it, respect the sacrifices made by the wives, made in terms of their health, their beauty, respect their home maker position, the sacrifices made by them in their career, for the sake of the families so on and so forth. Give small, but precious gifts to satisfy the wives Don't praise other ladies in their presence, but instead add **the flattery, 'like you she is'.** Respect their beauty and the liking of their sarees, saying face to face appreciations and needed suggestions, for their dress. If these are sincerely followed, the family wellness will be intact.

Problems Viewed from Another Dimension

A man of late 40' s, went to his favourite class teacher, nearing 90s, for the solution to the 'problems' faced in his life. He was in turn, asked to go to the high school, where he studied The following were the instructions given to him:-

"Get your school register, note down the names of your classmates and try to get the details about their present status. After getting those information, meet me"

He did accordingly.

There were more than 120 names in it. Upon hectic try, he could contact only half of those. Out of those 60,

- ***15 were not alive***
- ***7 were single and 13 were separated from their spouses***
- ***10 were drug or alcohol addicts, not worth to be pursued***
- ***5 were too poor to be mentioned***
- ***6 turned out to be so wealthy, to his surprise***
- ***Some were cancerous, some were paralyzed, diabetic, asthmatic or heart patients…***
- ***A couple of people were bed ridden with major ailments***
- ***The children of some were useless to their families***
- ***One was a criminal***
- ***One was looking for a life partner, after three separations***

Within a month, he could gather the above details of his peers and he met his teacher.

The teacher asked:- "Now tell me, how about your problem?"

The gentleman understood that he had no major health issues, he had sufficient funds, perfect mind, good family …

He realized that in this world, where many of his peers were facing some problem or the other, he is lucky to be leading a satisfactory and contented life.

The advice given by the teacher is worth to be followed by all:

- ***Give up the habit of comparing with others***
- ***All have their own destiny, still, if you think that you are in depression, then you should also go to your school, get the school register and………***
- ***Be contented and happy with whatever given by God and be grateful to Him.***

For Parents

The bottom line is – Do not prepare the road for the children: Rather prepare them for the road.

A Real Life Incident:-

- There was a very brilliant boy; he always scored 100% in Science.
- Got Selected for a premier Engineering Institute and scored excellent marks.
- Went to a reputed University in USA for MBA.
- Got a high paying job in America and settled there.
- Married a beautiful Tamil girl.
- Owned a palatial house and luxury cars.
- He had everything that made him successful, but........... after 15 years of coming to US, he committed suicide, after shooting his wife and children.

What Went Wrong?

This was taken for a research study in a noted research institute in USA.

The researcher met the boy's friends and family, found that he lost his job due to the country's economic crisis at that time. He had to sit without a job for a long time. Even after compromising his previous salary, he could not get any job His EMI for his housing loan, could not be paid and he lost it. They survived for a few months with less money. He and his wife together decided, to commit suicide. He first shot his wife and children, then shot himself.

The researcher concluded that:

- ***The man was programmed for only brighter side of life, but he was not trained for handling adverse situations.***
- ***Parents should prepare their children for facing failures with courage.***

Some more useful insights brought out by the research were:-

1. More emphasis is given to successful habits. Success and failures are two sides of the coin. Nobody knows about the next crisis. Best success habit lies in making oneself, ready for even failures.' **Do your best, but be prepared for the worst'** should be the manthra.

2. Parents should teach their wards about how money works, instead of teaching them, to work for money. Help them in finding their passion, because these degrees will not help them, in the next economic crisis and we don't know when the next crisis will hit the world

3. Success is a lousy teacher. Failure teaches you more. The parents should not only enable their wards to acquire IQ, (Intelligence Quotient) EQ, (Emotional Quotient) SQ (Spiritual quotient) but also AQ, the adversity quotient, preparing them to face failures.

4. Different Quotients, to be kept in mind, by the parents, with regard to bringing up of their children are:-

   Intelligence Quotient (IQ)

   Emotional Quotient (EQ)

   Social Quotient (SQ)

a. ***Intelligence Quotient (IQ):*** this is the measure of your comprehension ability, to solve mathematics, memorize things and recall subject matters.

b. ***Emotional Quotient (EQ):*** this is the measure of your ability, to maintain **peace** with others; keep to time; be responsible; be honest; respect boundaries; be humble, genuine and considerate.

c. ***Social Quotient (SQ):*** this is the measure of your ability, to build a network of friends and maintain it, over a long period of time.

People who have higher EQ and SQ, tend to go farther in life, than those who have high IQ ,low EQ and SQ. Most schools capitalize in improving IQ level while EQ and SQ are down played.

A man of high IQ can end up, being employed by a man of high EQ and SQ, even though he has an average IQ.

EQ represents one's character; **SQ represents one's charisma.** Teach the children, the habits, which will improve these three Qs, but more especially EQ and SQ.

EQ and SQ make one manage better than the other.

5. ***Now there is a 4th one:***

The Adversity Quotient **(AQ):** the measure of your ability, to go through a rough path in life and come out, without losing your mind.

AQ determines who will not face the troubles, who will abandon their family or who will consider suicide.

Spiritual Quotient (SpQ):- Not undermined, but this should be gradually inculcated, when all the above four are acquired, they will have the mind to adopt this Q ,at a later stage.

Therefore parents have to expose their children to specific areas of life, other than academic. They should engage them in manual work, without terming them, as a sort of punishment. Develop their EQ, SQ and AQ. They should become multifaceted human beings, being able to do things, independently.

The bottom line is – Do not prepare the road for the children. Rather, prepare them for the road

Care or Control?

There is one more aspect which parents should keep in mind.

A counsellor was consulted by a middle age couple. In front of him, they started fighting with words. The upset husband said 'See doc… I 'care' so much for her, but she does not respect me'. The wife immediately jumped at him ' sorry, you don't care for me, but just control me'

The care from one person was perceived as control by another!

What is care and what is control? How to identify them?

A confession from a father will throw more light on this:-

- *I had a heated argument with my college – going daughter, over a petty matter. Strong and hot words were exchanged. Both of us were in distressed mood.*
- *When the situation cooled down, we started speaking to each other. "Dad! I know you became hot, with the simple reason that*

your instructions were overlooked by me, not because I went wrong. That was the flash point.

- *I was taken aback by her honest and very genuine feedback. More control was apparently visible than my care, which was masked. Parents expose more control than care*
- *A genuine care will not make her angry or disturbed towards me but instead it will explore ways to make us corrected.*
- *If I am finding it difficult, to cope with any relationship, I need to closely analyse if there is any subtle control, masked behind my evident care, because care is an expression of love, while control is an expression of ego…*
- *Control cuts. Care connects.*
- *Control hurts. Care heals*
- *Keep caring for children, but don't control them because, often parents are not wrong, they are just ' dissimilar '*

Is not a worthy advice for all parents, rather for any dual relationship?

For Younger Generation

Younger generations, who compare their belongings – home, car, bank balance etc – with their friends and relatives, should ponder over this wonderful explanation

Who is Rich? Who is Poor?

To the question, if there are any measure for richness, a beautiful answer is given, with the most appropriate examples, by a commerce student. Here is his answer:-

When I was doing my B. Com, there was a Professor teaching 'Economics'. His lectures were very interesting, since he had an interesting way to drive home each and every concept

One day, in the class, he asked the following questions:-

1. *Define zero and infinity?*

2. *Can zero and infinity be identical?*

We all thought that we knew the answers and we replied as follows:-

Zero means nothing. Infinity means a number, greater than any countable number. Zero and Infinity are opposite and they can never be the same. He contradicted us, by first talking about infinity and asked how can there be any number, which is greater than any countable number? We had no answers.

He then explained the concept of infinity, in a very interesting way, which I remember even after 30 years. He asked to us to imagine, that there is an illiterate farmer, who can count only up to 30. Now, if the number of cows he has, is less than 30 and you ask him, how many cows he has he can tell you the precise number (like 5, 9, 25, etc.).

However, if the number is more than 30, he is likely to say 'more'. He then explained that in science, infinity means 'too many' (and not uncountable) and in the same way zero means 'too few' (and not nothing). As an example, he said that, if we take the diameter of the Earth as compared to distance between Earth and Sun, the diameter of earth can be said to be zero, since it is too small. However, when we compare the same diameter of earth with the size of a grain, diameter of earth can be said to be infinite. So,, he concluded, that the same thing can be **Zero** and **Infinity**, at the same time, depending on the context, or your matrix of comparison

Extrapolating this concept of Infinity and Zero, to Richness and Poverty, he further concluded that:-

- *It all depends on the scale of comparison with our wants. If our income is more than our wants, we are rich, if our wants are more than our income, we are poor.*
- *I consider myself rich because my wants are far less than my income.*
- *I have become rich, not so much by acquiring lots of money, but by progressively reducing my wants. If I can reduce my wants, I too can become rich, at the present moment.*

Younger generations, who compare their belongings – home, car, bank balance etc – with their friends and relatives, should ponder over this wonderful explanation. Let all our lives get rich by good thoughts, good deeds and good people around us always.

Please ponder over the following:-

- *In the 60s, a Car was a luxury.*
- *In the 70s, a Television was a luxury.*
- *In the 80s, a Telephone was a luxury.*
- *In the 90s, a Computer was a luxury...*

- *Luxury is no more a foreign tour and eating food in a five star hotel*
- *It is consuming home grown vegetables from the terrace*
- *Luxury is not in providing lift to your house*
- *It is the ability to go up to 5–6 stories without lift*
- *Luxury is not the ability to afford a costly refrigerator and eat frozen foods.*
- *It is the ability to eat freshly cooked food, 2–3 times a day.*
- *Luxury is not having a home theatre system and watching the famous movies or serials*
- *It is physically experiencing good natural beauty*
- *Luxury is not getting treatment from the most expensive hospital in the area*
- *It is living without any major diseases or physical ailment*

  What is luxury, then?

- ***It is being healthy, being happy, leading a happy married life, having an affectionate family, being with loving friends, living in an unpolluted place***

  That is the ultimate luxury in the present context

It would be apt and worthwhile, if the present day generation people, follow the above in letter and spirit.

Having seen about the material richness, it is better, to talk about the perceived beauty.

Real Beauty

In a spiritual meet, the teacher had conversation with a 25 year old youth. It went like this:

"If you sight a gorgeous girl in a beach, what will be your immediate action?"

"I will start admiring her beauty"

"After that girl has crossed, will you look back too?"

"yes"

"Tell me, how long will you recognize that girl's face?"

"May be for 30 minutes until another beautiful face appears."

Teacher said to the youth 'Assume that you are assigned a job by me. I gave you a bunch of holy books and said that bunch should be delivered to a very rich and prominent person in a specific area. You went to his house to deliver that. When you saw his house, you came to know that, he was a highly respected person in that area. Handed over that… He got the books from you. Then, when you started to leave the place, you were asked to come inside and he gave a warm reception with nice eatables… He also arranged a vehicle to drop you at your place"

"Now tell me, how long will you remember that gentleman?"

The young man said "I will never forget that person in my life"

Addressing the gathering through the youth, the teacher said "This is the reality of life."

"Gorgeous face is remembered for a while and forgotten after a few moment, but nice behavior is retained in mind for life."

Concentrate on the beauty of your behavior, more than the beauty of your face and body. Life will become enjoyable for yourself unforgettable and inspirational for others…

This is the supreme lesson the present day younger generation, should learn.

The Tenth Apple Effect

A hungry man who was longing for food, saw an apple tree. He took one apple. It was very tasty. Took one more. Liked it. Third, fourth, fifth………so on. He could realize that the liking and taste were diminishing, as he consumed more. With the tenth apple, he took and threw it away. It was no longer needed. This is an example of **Diminishing Marginal Utility, which states that, as consumption of a particular commodity increases, it will result in less and lesser utility. Utility means happiness, contentment, and gratitude. Marginal utility, is the increase of the above factors. Material possessions can satisfy one up to a certain extent, beyond which his contentment diminishes.**

Apart from the above insights, it is imperative that we should not forget that we should be grateful to the giver who started giving the commodity. Just as the tenth apple was thrown, gratitude should not be.

Having seen more useful concepts for couples, parents, youth etc., we are going to see a very common factor, that affects the mutual relationship. This is termed as Perceptual Filter.

Filters Separate

If everybody starts changing himself or herself, the whole world will change. This is the greatest lesson we have to learn in this world.

Perceptual Filters

What are these perceptual filters? Let us analyze that, using an anecdote from the Epic Ramayana:

The Great Epic Ramayana was originally written by the Rishi Vaalmiki.

Based on this, many started writing different versions of Ramayana. One such was by Thulasidasa. It is believed that after writing the entire episodes, Thulasi Das was reciting verbatim to Lord Anjaneya and the Lord was attentively listening to each and every verse. On one occasion, it was Lord Himself who happened to be one of the characters. 'HE goes to Ashokvan and sees Sita there' thus go the verses. Until then, there was no dispute. But when Thulasi Das recited 'Anjaneya saw white flowers falling from Asoka tree' HE objected to it.' I saw only red flowers how could you say that they were white?' He argued. Thulasidasa was harping on his stand-only white. They went to Lord Rama to resolve the issue. After hearing patiently from both, Rama said both were right. How it could be? Rama clarified that Anjaneya, went with anger in his eyes and hence the white flower looked red through his red colored eyes. The original color as imagined by Thulasidasa, was only white. Because of the anger, on the part of Anjaneya, it was appearing red. Lord Anjaneya had the filter of anger in his eyes that made the color appear as red. This incident was the one that happened in Thretha Yuga (Ramayana period)

In the Dwapara Yuga (Mahabharatha period) different characters were using different filters and each one, was justifying his stand, based on the perceptions they had, towards the persons or things they came across.

It was with the **filter of bondage** towards his sons, the king *Dhritarashtra* was siding with his son, Duryodhana in all his actions, despite the fact, that the latter was wrong in his approach towards his brothers Pandavas.

It was with the **filter of *contempt*** that Duryodhana was employing, in all his actions against Pandavas.

It was with the **filter of *hatred*** towards Hasthinapura, all actions of uncle *Saguni* were based upon.

It was with the **filter of *loyalty,*** towards his kingdom Pithamaga Bheeshma acted upon, irrespective of whether all his actions were right or wrong

It was with the filter of ***affection,*** towards his son, Ashwaththama, *Dronacharya* pinned all his actions.

It was with the **filter of gratitude,** towards his friend Duryodhana, Karna made all his moves.

It was with the **filter of *vengeance*** towards his early childhood friend, Drona, King Drupada acted upon.

The whole of Epic Mahabharatha was thus centering around different perceptual filters used by the major characters.

It repeats in the present **Yuga of Kali too**. A newly married couple was occupying a new flat. On the first day, when they were having their breakfast, the wife saw her neighbor hang the wash. "See the laundry! It is not clean. She either does not know how to wash, or she does not use the right washing powder. Anyhow the fault is with her only". Not a day passed without those comments. Every time, the husband was giving only a silence as his answer.

On one Sunday, the husband got up earlier and the wife, after getting up later, called her husband and said "see the laundry is very clean today. At last she has learnt to clean properly."

The husband, this time, gave a straight answer "I got up earlier today and cleaned our window. It was very dirty."

This is true, for many of us. What we see, when we watch people, depends on the filter we use in our window, called mind. That color leads to our perception. The world we see, is not the actual world, but the world we see through the filter we employ in our window called mind... The lady, in the quoted example, had the color of the window as the ***blaming tendency*** towards her neighbour. Before we pass on any criticism, it may be a good idea to check our state of mind and ask ourselves whether our window is pure or colored, with any biased attitude. Most of us are wearing colored glasses with our own prejudices, preferences and see the world through that colored window.

A husband or wife with the color of the filter as the suspicion, will always look into each and every act of the other with some ulterior motive.

A child having a filter of frustration, towards his or her working parents always thinks they don't care for him/her.

A manager who has a filter of apathy, towards his/her subordinate, will always find fault with the latter.

A worker with the filter of negative attitude, towards the management will behave with disloyalty.

A citizen who has the filter of cynical attitude towards his government, will view each and every act of the government as deceiving, however good it may be.

A party which has a jealous attitude towards another, will find fault with each and every act of the other, however genuine it may be.

A jaundiced eye will see the entire world as yellow. An angered eye will see the entire world as red. It is not the true color of the world, through which we view things, but only with the filter, we employ.

It is not that, one uses, only one filter, all the times. Sometimes one filter, at a different occasion, an entirely a different one, depending upon the attitude towards the concerned.

A supervisor who blames his boss, is using the filter of subordination, at the same when finding fault with his worker, has the filter of authority. A daughter in law, uses the filter of favor on the part of her own mother and the filter of contempt for her mother-in-law. The converse is also true. A mother-in-law who suppresses her daughter-in-law uses the filter of authority and the same lady uses the filter of affection for her own daughter. A central government employee uses the filter of contempt, when he points out the poor services by a state government employee or at the same token, one department of state or central government employee looks at the other department with the filter of blame game. When it is turned against him, he uses the filter of defence. Instances like these, in our practical life can be multiplied.

The color of the filter, that is inside us, will only come out, through all our actions.

Change your Filters

It is not the world that has to be changed, but the way we look at the same, has to be. It is not the world we have to change, but the filter we employ on various occasions.

When a king was suffering from a specific disease,, his health advisor told him to change everything, he saw into green. He ordered the minister to arrange for the same. A saint on hearing this, came to him and told him" why you spent so much money for this change? Do like this. Wear the green spectacle and it will make everything appear green.". The king realized that and did accordingly. Instead of changing the world, it is better to change oneself.

The Above Concept can also be Explained with Two Anecdotes

First, Michael Gorbachev, the then premier, wanted to change radically the then United Russia, USSR and it was a miserable failure. A joke was there around that change. An unemployed youth was standing in a long queue waiting to get wheat, in a ration shop. Suddenly he withdrew from the queue and asked his neighbor to take care of his seat, since he had to go and finish an important task. He said he would come and join again in the queue. Till that time, the queue would not move, he told very confidently. The neighbor asked him what was the most important job other than getting wheat from the ration shop. He replied "killing Gorbachev" and he left. After fifteen minutes, he returned. On questioning by the neighbor, whether he was able to achieve the mission, he replied, there was still a longer queue, waiting at the place of Gorbachev to kill him. The queue at the ration shop, was indeed better. From that day onwards, he said he was going to change himself. It was better to change him than attempting to change the world, he could realize.

Second, an old man in his death bed, was surrounded by his entire relatives. He was asked to share his piece of advice to be followed by all:

He said-" when I was twenty, I ventured to change the world. At only forty, I realized it was a futile attempt. Then I thought I can try to change my own country. I reached sixty without any success. Then

I spent another twenty years attempting to change my village and family without any result. Now only, I realize that I should have changed myself. It is a late realization and dear children don't repeat the mistake of mine. Change yourself first".

If everybody starts changing himself or herself, the whole world will change. This is the greatest lesson we have to learn in this world.

Filters Change Our Color

A learned person was teaching his students. He asked one student, to have a cup of coffee in his hand. He asked another student to go and dash gently against his shoulder He did and the coffee splashed on the floor. He asked the students why the coffee splashed. The answer came uniformly, that one student shoved with the coffee in hand. He shook the other's shoulder etc etc. The learned was not convinced. He asked further, if there was tea inside, what would have happened. The tea would have splashed, came the uniform answer. If it was a cool drink – for the question they answered that the cool drink would have splashed. If there was nothing inside, then? No splash, was the answer. He concluded, it was not the shaking of the shoulder or shoving the person, that splashed the coffee… It was because of the simple reason, that coffee was inside and that alone splashed outside. If it was tea, tea would have splashed and cool drink and so on. What is inside will only splash. Life is like a shake or shoving. It will make the thing inside us to splash, if it is joy, love, kindness or compassion, it will come out. If it is anger jealousy, hatred, and it will come out. What is inside is more important. The fault is not the shaking of the shoulder, or shoving of the person. It is because of what is inside. The learned person concluded.

The color of the filter, that is inside us, will only come out through all of our actions. Let us all use all positive and optimistic filters, make the world a pleasant one, drive ourselves to be happier.

Settings

Weeds and Seeds in Relationship

It is not the question of this or that. It is one of the examples of this and that. We want both - emotional reserves and realistic expectations, for better relations and productive results.

Weeds and Seeds

When we start growing a particular seed in a specific soil, along with the seeds, the weeds will also grow. It should be our endeavour, to eliminate the weeds, so that the faster growth of the seeds, will be seen. If not, weeds will grow, hampering the growth of the seeds. What is applicable for the plant, will be applicable for the relationship as well. We will have both seeds – things conducive for relationship, and weeds-affecting badly the relationship. Let us see one positive and negative example on these lines

Family Relationship

That was his daughter's birth day. Ragav had promised his wife Mohana and his 4 year old daughter Smitha for an outing, during that evening. It was agreed, that he would come by 6pm, all to go to a restaurant and then to the beach. Smitha was at the peak of her joy, with all the natural expectations of that tender age. She had got herself ready at 5 itself. Sitting at the entrance with her eyes on the road, the little one was eagerly awaiting her dad." Why this dad is not coming?"Every ten minutes she had been pestering her mother, who said 'He will come! Wait!'. Though her tongue uttered those words, with her 8 years of experience as Ragav's wife, Mohana's inner mind was telling the negative, though she did not spell it openly. "Why should I disappoint the kid?"

Time was rolling. It was 6... 7...even 8 passed, without the sight of the dad. The poor kid went to bed, eyes filled with tears, mind full of disappointments and stomach empty. Mohana was totally fed up. These kinds of experiences were not uncommon for her. During the 8 years of her married life, she had been getting hundreds of excuses from Ragav for not fulfilling his promises – heavy work at office, client calls, meeting with boss ....so on and so forth. She had become accustomed to his behaviour. Though she would invariably be trying to bury her anger, sometimes it did find out an outlet.

"Had he ever bothered to care about my sentiments?" Mohana was trying to recollect her past... It would be very much natural, for a newly married lady like Mohana to be longing to go for outings, with the husband But, in the case of Ragav, his first wife would always be his job and he never cared for her sentiments – that kind of feeling had gone into her subconscious mind. Her pent up emotions did find an outlet on their first marriage anniversary day, when her parents were there around. He promised to go to the temple followed by dinner at a restaurant – all went into the air. He came at 10. 30 totally spoiling her mood. The day, which ought to have been very memorable and pleasant ended with bitter memories. Her parents left on the next day early morning, without talking to their son-in-law. The workaholic husband was not able to convince his wife, for his delay on that previous evening. His close friend got involved in a worst accident and he was held up at the hospital, for rendering the needed help. When he narrated the actual reason, Mohana did not have the mind to believe his statements. Even on that fateful day, when she had a miscarriage, he never turned up to the hospital. Her parents felt very sad, for marrying their daughter to such an irresponsible, incorrigible son-in-law. Such was the kind of mistrust, he had built in, over the years and also the confidence level, he had developed towards his better half.

Factory Relationship

There were heated arguments in the conference hall of that company, Aruna Auto Components. The wage revision talks had not come to any amicable settlement. From both the sides - the site chief, known for his arrogance and rigidity and the union leader with his entire negative attitude towards the site chief - there were no signs of any compromise. They were harping on the same point, without any further improvement... Kumar, the HR manager was often intervened to ease the situation. The peak of the heated arguments reached with the forceful dragging of a paper weight on the table, by the site chief, which accidentally flew and hit at the hand of the union leader. That was enough. All the office bearers joined together and they were about to man handle the site chief. Kumar had cleverly pushed the chief to the adjoining hall and gently put his hands on the right shoulder of the union leader,

"Did he throw it at you purposefully? Come on! Let us go to my cabin! Cool down! We will continue the discussion later. Please follow me"

There was silence! "Don't you believe me? Please come"

"Ok! Sir! We respect you and your words. We would not have joined this talk, without your presence" all followed Kumar. What should have become a very awkward and untoward incident, was very cleverly averted by the presence (of mind) of Kumar.

Kumar had stamped his name all around the company, within a very short period of his joining. Whenever any conflict cropped up, he would be there to address the workers and he would see that, it got resolved amicably. He would be rigid as well as flexible, as the situations demand-rigid in his principle, flexible in the relationship.

"Let us go to Kumar sir! He will definitely give the right solution". He would be present to rescue any employee, during the crisis

"Let us not take this issue to him. This case is very weak. He won't yield" Workers also knew that he would not yield that much easily and he would be very assertive.

"Why should we bother? Kumar sir is there!. He will give a better option." Such was the confidence level he had developed with the employees.

The company which was once notorious for its IR (industrial relations) problems, had become an island of peace, after his entry. Even the most indisciplined worker would surrender in his presence, due to his tactics and persuasive power.

No wonder, he was able to cool down the union leader in the situation mentioned above... Such was his personal power, which he had built up over a period of time. His close relationship with the employees, outside his office, made him closer to their mind and heart.

Let us set aside the above two situations for a while and peep into some management concepts.

There is a Leadership Theory, taught in management, called Managerial Grid developed by Robert R. Blake and Jane Mouton. It talks about Task and People orientation. A leader has to strike a balance between people and the task to be completed, for maximum output as well as for harmonious relationship.

This can also be explained by two mutually exclusive factors, in respect of relationship building – viz emotional reserves and expectations. We can compare emotional reserves with seeds and deposits, expectations with weeds and withdrawals. The author is attempting to revisit the above Grid Theory by replacing task with expectations, people with emotional reserves.

Expectations are the obligations we look in, from our significant others and the emotional reserves are the harmonious relationship, or the emotional bonding we have developed with them, over a period of time. If the reserves are more, obligations will be fulfilled smoothly. When the former is less and the latter is more, there will be hesitations in meeting out the obligations or carrying out the assigned task and it will lead to issues in relationship. This can be compared to the analogies with the seeds and weeds in a garden and also the deposits and withdrawals in a bank. Seeds here represent the upkeep and maintenance of the plant, amidst the unwanted growth of weeds. If there are more weeds and there is no or less attempt to remove, the growth of the plant will be affected. In the same way, when the deposits are more than the withdrawals, there will be surplus cash balance. If less, it will erode the balance.

What is applied in plants or banks, can also be applicable in our relationship. When we plant the seeds of trust, by the care, concern and help for the significant others, the misunderstanding, the weeds, cropping up every now and then, are also removed periodically. When this trust, the seeds, become less, the misunderstanding, or the weeds, creep in and the relationship will be affected.

When the deposits accumulate, the periodic withdrawals won't affect the balance much. In the relationship banking, the emotional reserves – the deposits, made often, will take care of the periodic withdrawals – issues or concerns or misunderstanding. For a harmonious relationship, be it in family or business, this emotional reserves have to be maintained on a constant and continuous basis-no let up at any point of time. The family or business leader has to keep an eye on this and be vigilant over any possible lapses.

We can see certain teachers in institutions, family leaders or managers in organizations, in which, with their built – in emotional reserves, will be able to get things done easily, simultaneously maintaining a smooth relationship. Their significant others won't get offended, even when they are taken to task by their concerned leaders. Such is the emotional bonding between them. On the other hand, it is not possible for many, to extract work,/meet out the obligations, from their significant others, because of the less or absence of emotional bonding, they failed to create.

In the family example quoted above, the emotional reserves are less in the relationship, between the couple – Ragav and Mohana. The past experiences of Mohana with her husband Ragav, indicate the growth of more weeds of misunderstanding, than the seeds of trust. There were more withdrawals or unrealistic assumptions/ expectations, taken for granted by the workaholic husband, Ragav. The deposits – building confidence, fulfilling the promises made and striking a work life balance etc – are very less.

With the factory example quoted above, Kumar, the HR Manager has built up enough emotional reserves and there is no wonder, his expectations are met without any relationship issues. It was the reverse in the case of the site chief. The seeds of trust planted by Kumar were sufficient enough, to get rid of the weeds cropping up periodically. The deposits of confidence building, were huge and the workers don't even mind about fulfilling his reasonable expectations-the withdrawals.

In today's world – be it family, societal or business relationship – one should not overlook either the emotional reserves or the expectations. One without the other will not serve the purpose. Excessive reserves, without any expectations will lead to domination by one side and unrealistic expectations without sufficient emotional reserves will lead to spoiling of the relationship.

It is not the question of this or that. It is one of the examples of this and that. We want both – emotional reserves and realistic expectations for better relations and productive results.

'Contact' and 'Connect' in Relationship

Many are confusing these two and they tend to interchange them. It would be better if we understand the differences between these two, for proper application in our mutual relationship. Let us explain this with an anecdote:

And IT professional from Bangalore had an interaction with a renowned Spiritual Guru. The dialogue went like this:

IT professional – "Sir, Can you explain the difference between Connect and Contact about which you talked in your lecture last week? I am not clear about that.

Without any direct answer, the Guru asked him," Are you from Bangalore?"

IT professional: "yes"

Guru: "Who are there at home?"

Getting perturbed, the IT professional said. "Father had expired. Mother is there. Three sisters and a brother. All are well settled and married"

The Guru with a smile on his face, without giving the answer to the asked question, again questioned "Do you often talk to your mother?"

The IT professional looked visibly irritated said" rarely"

The Guru: "When did you talk to her last?"

"May be a month ago."

"Do your brothers and sisters meet often? When did you meet last as a family gathering?"

At this point, IT professional had sweated heavily. It was as if the Guru was cross examining the IT professional.

The IT professional said, "We all met two years back at a family function"

The Guru: "How long did you all stay together?"

The IT professional after having a glass of water said, "two days…"

Guru: "Ok! How long did you sit together with your mother?"

The IT professional, looking very sad, started twisting his shirt buttons.

The Guru: "Did you have at least a square meal with her? Did you ask how she is? Did you ask how her days are passing after your father's death?"

Drops of tears were falling from the eyes of the IT professional. The Guru took hold of the hands of the IT professional and said: "Don't get angry with me, or get upset or sad. I am sorry if I have hurt you unknowingly… But this is basically the answer, to your question about "Contact and Connect." You have 'Contact' with your mother but you don't have 'Connect' with her. You are not connected to her. Connection is between heart and heart…

Staying together, sharing meals and caring for each other, touching, shaking hands, having eye contact in spending some time together… All you brothers and sisters have 'Contact' but no 'Connection' with each other…"

The IT professional wiped his rolling tears and said: "Thanks for teaching me a fine and unforgettable lesson."

Whether at home or in the society, this is what happens. Technology might have done wonders, brought people together virtually. But it has separated them in their hearts. We may have friends through Face book, LinkedIn or Whatsapp. The fact is that friendship is not real. During crisis those FB/Linkedin/Whatsapp friends won't come to our rescue at all. Even in family, we don't talk to each other directly. We do through Whatsapp messages. We don't even remember the mobile number of our kith and kin. We have to immediately refer to the mobile. This is how our relationship exists. Nothing is in our hearts. Everything is through the gadget.

It is the valuable lesson, not only for the IT professional, but also for all the younger generation.

Non Passing on to the Next...

Leave alone the relationship with our kith and kin: how is our relationship with our neighbors? See the comparison of the present generation, with the old. Old is always gold.

We have crossed the following village life styles of our senior citizens in their generation, but it is a pity, those were not passed on to the next generation:

Here is the groaning from a senior citizen:-

Even amidst poverty, we were generous to our neighbors. We would give the special food prepared by us, to our neighbors and the loaned vessel would not be returned empty: it would carry some thing special or other from their side. If our kitchen garden gave drumstick, it would be shared with our friend circle and the raw banana from theirs would come to us. There were occasions, when the neighbor's small child would come for curd and we would go to them, for coffee powder, during emergency. The remains, after making rice and dhal would be given to the maids in our village, for which they would exchange with the cow dung.

If we come out, taking the hurricane lamp, during night, the villagers would become panic, start enquiring about our health. When coming after tour, coffee, sambar, rasam, butter milk would be delivered by our neighbours, on the first day of the return. Furniture would be exchanged for the functions – be it marriage or death. For marriages, excepting the cooking jobs, all major tasks would be shouldered by the villagers. On those days, holidays, would be declared for all the kitchens in that area. For the marriages and other functions, ladies would temporarily exchange their golden ornaments to the close friends. If we go to get milk, from the vendors, for the child in our house, they won't accept money for the same.

In a family with more siblings, the old dress would be passed on to the younger ones. The farmers would have their pump sets, in the paddy field, for irrigation purposes. Anybody can go there and take bath. For the villagers, that water, falling from the pipe line, would be the courtallam falls.

Though their cash box may not be full, their mind would always be rich.

Now it is the opposite. Cash is plenty, but the loving kindness is empty

Wordings are the Same, Meaning......?

Everybody passes from one stage to other in his or her life cycle. The same words used by us, will have different meaning, at different phases of our life. If we understand those meaning in letter and spirit, the Bliss and Peace in our relationship will be abundant. What money cannot bring, these words with their subtle meaning will. See those words ....

For a small girl, a small boy is ***BF – means Best Friend***

For a teen aged girl, the same ***BF – Boy Friend***

When they are married and get a baby, the same BF to her, is ***Baby's Father***

When they become old, the old man says to the old lady same BF – Now it is ***Be For ever***

At the death bed, the same to her – BF – ***Bye For ever***

Before her death, she murmurs to the husband, at the memorial – BF here means – ***Be For you***

Age may pass, but the real love will, and should, remain the same. That is the secret of any family wellness or for that matter of any relationship.

Reflections:-

Reflections:-

Career Wellness

Having wisdom, is more important than having logic. And wisdom comes from experience, not from books

Recap

We have thus far, seen the three wellness – Physical, Mental, Family. Physical wellness is no doubt is primary. But without financial wellness or Career wellness, other wellness will lose their significance. To take an analogy, in any organisation the generation of money is made through marketing department which only feeds all the other departments. That in no way will amount to say that all other departments are lesser important. In the same way, career or financial wellness is the source of income for any individual with which all other wellness depend upon. Udyogam Purusha Lakshnam – as the adage goes in Sanskrit, meaning – for a male, job will alone give the status. In this modern world, when both male and female are working for their livelihood, the importance of career cannot be undermined. Thiraikadal odiyum thiraviyam thedu, as the adage in Tamil says, one has to go abroad and earn money. The fundamental premise with which career wellness **exists is** the money earned, is not only for the individual and it should be used for helping the needy. If we help others, we take up the work of God. In turn HE will multiply our income. Because, as The Holy Bible says, it is in giving that we receive, as we sow abundantly, we reap abundantly. That is the Universal law. Only thing, the money earned should be by ethical and legal means.

Positive Attitude Towards Money

In this connection, it is apt to quote a few incidents from the life of Vidhyaranya, the 12th Jagathguru of Sri Sharadha Peedam of Shringeri. He was the patron Saint and the king maker of Vijayanagara Samrajya during 14th AD. He was a poor bachelor and no girl was ready to marry him. He did strenuous penance against the Goddess Lakshmi, the Goddess for wealth (who poured gold, to the poor brahmin lady, when Adi Shankara, recited Kanagadhara Sthothram to seek the Goddess' Blessings, for that poor brahmin lady.)

Goddess appeared before him and said that he was not blessed enough to become rich at that birth and for that he had to wait for the next birth. Though he was upset, his friend gave the idea, that becoming a Sanyasi would amount to take another birth. Accordingly, he became a Sanyasi and again prayed to the Goddess. The Goddess granted him a huge wealth. Then that Sanyasi thought, what those precious wealth would mean for a Sanyasi like him. It was during that time, Hoysala Kingdom (the present Karnataka) had been invaded by the Moghul King Malik Kapoor. That Sanyasi, with the huge wealth with him and with his motivation of two archins, who were looking after the cattle herd, powered them, made them fight against the Moghul King. It was the background story of the establishment of the great Vijayanagara Empire. When wealth was with him, that Sanyasi instead of disowning made use of them to liberate the country from the clutches of a foreign invasion. The money was in the safe hands and utilised for a noble purpose.

One more incident occurred in the last century. John D. Rock Feller, the noted rich man and a philanthropist was once travelling in a flight. One co passenger asked him why he should suffer at that old age?. Why not take rest? Rock Feller asked him, what they were doing then. Smooth travel in the flight, was the answer. Can we ask the pilot, to stop the engine and take rest, since the travel being smooth. To this question, the co passenger told him, all would be in danger. Rock Feller very cleverly told him, that same would be the case with him. He would be in danger, if he were taking rest, since he always wished to be very active. Moreover the major portion of the money earned would be used for charity.

The common thread that pervades through the above two incidents is that we should earn more money not for ourselves but for helping the needy – the country, during the foreign invasion, in the first case and in the second case, the needy poor people, for whom, much help was needed.

The moral from the two incidents is:

We should develop positive attitude towards money and other material things: that should be utilised for helping the needy.

While these talk about the positive attitude, we have to develop, the dare necessity to have enough money in this world of uncertainty cannot be overlooked. A new Harvard research says that money is not for luxuries and many wants. It helps people to avoid many of the day-to-day hassles, that cause stress. Money can put us at ease, preparing us to be ready for the unexpected and unforeseen circumstances. It will surely free us from certain worries. But, it is worthwhile to caution about a situation.

See the above picture:-

This is called SISI Syndrome – Single Income, Single Identity.

A mouse was put at the top of a jar filled with grains. It was too happy, to find so much of food around. It need not go anywhere, since the food is readily available without the necessity of searching for it.

But, alas, in a few days, the level of the grains, became diminished. Moreover, it was trapped and it could not come out of it. It had to solely depend upon someone to put grains in the same jar to survive. It might even not get the grain of its choice. If it had to live,, it had to feed on whatever had been put into the jar. Such was the pitiable condition of the mouse.

Here are the valuable lessons, learnt from this:

- *Convincing with the short term pleasures will make one trapped permanently.*
- *Being in a comfort zone, will make one suffer, for survival.*
- *Un utilization of potential will lead to the loss of it.*
- *If proper and right actions are not taken, it would be highly impossible to come out of the difficult situation.*

With our sincere efforts, we have to make money in an ethical and a legal way. There should not be any contentment attitude for earning money. If we have the attitude,' that the money earned, is not only for me, but for the needy', then our perceptions towards money will be more positive and it will push us to earn more

Career wellness, if pursued well, will enable us, to earn more. That requires more systematic and sincere efforts. It cannot come all on a sudden. Rome cannot be built in a single day. Be it our own business, or our career uplifting, while working for somebody, success requires a lot of concerted efforts, hard as well as smart work. Many see only the final success. It is never linear, but, has many curves, twists and turns.

Logic or Wisdom

In that pursuit for success, whether one requires logic or wisdom? The answer to this pertinent question is given by the following dialogue between a youth and a Guru:

A young man in his thirties, knocks at the door of a spiritual Guru. He says: "Can you please teach Vedas?"His very body language is not liked by the Guru.

"Are you comfortable with Sanskrit and our ancient system??" the Guru asks.

"No – for both. I am sure, it won't matter. I have just completed my thesis on Logic at a reputed university in USA. I am of the firm opinion that with that knowledge it is possible" his body language again irritates the Guru.

The Guru asks him to undergo a test on Logic. If he passes, he can be taught Vedas. The young man agrees for that.

The test begins with the following question. "Two men come out of a chimney. One with a clean face; the other with a dirty face. Which one washes his face?"

To the question by the young "Is this, in fact a test on logic?", the Guru gave the affirmative.

"The one with the dirty face washes his face" – he gives the answer

"Wrong. The one with the clean face washes his face. Examine the logic. The one with the dirty face looks at the one, with the clean face and thinks his face is clean. The one with the clean face looks at the one with the dirty face and thinks his face is dirty. So, the one with the clean face washes his face."

"Oh, that nice," the young man says. "ok, put me under one more test"

The Guru repeats the same old question.

"Answer has been already given by you. The one with the clean face washes his face."

"Wrong. Each one washes his face. Examine the logic. The one with the dirty face looks at the one with the clean face and thinks his face is clean. The one with the clean face looks at the one with the dirty face and thinks his face is dirty. So, the one with the clean face washes his face. When the one with the dirty face sees the one with the clean face wash his face, he also washes his face. So, each one washes his face."

"I don't agree that, a man, like me, with a profound knowledge on logic can fail. Put me under another test.' 'retorted the egoistic young.

Same question again from the Guru.

"Each one washes his face." is the answer.

"Wrong. Neither one washes his face. Examine the logic. The one with the dirty face looks at the one, with the clean face and thinks his face is clean. The one with the clean face looks at the one with the dirty face and thinks his face is dirty. But when the one with the clean face sees the one with the dirty face doesn't wash his face, he also doesn't wash his face. So, neither one washes his face."

The young man is desperate to study Vedas and insists for one more test. Guru harps on the same question.

"Neither one washes his face." is the answer.

"Wrong. Do you now see, why logic is not conducive to study Vedas? Answer me, how is it possible, for two men, coming from the same chimney, one with a clean face and the other coming out dirty. Haven't you noticed that? If you seriously look into this question, it is absurd, without any common sense. If you spend your time, answering these kinds of silly questions, all your responses will also be silly.

He further added that it is not efficiency, which is doing things right, but effectiveness, which is doing the right thing, that will fetch the desired results. You should have given the straight forward answer, about the nature of this absurd, silly question, at the very first instance Moreover humility is the first thing that is needed for studying anything new, Vedas included.

The take away from this episode is – Having wisdom, is more important than having logic. And wisdom comes from experience, humility, willingness to learn, definitely, not from books. If we keep this in our mind, it would be a guiding factor, throughout our career.

Deserving to Desire

Sports, fitness, business and indeed Life are played on a 6-inch ground...the space between our own two ears!

Deserve First

All of us will have the desire to become rich, but the question is, ***Are we deserving for that***?

Without enhancing the deserving power, we cannot fulfill our desires. It will be emphasized, by the following story:

Long back, two travelers were moving from one place to another, by walk. Their destination had not come. Since it was getting dark, they decided to stay in a deserted bungalow on the way and spend the night there, proceed their journey, next day morning. They had brought some breads, which they decided to use for dinner. The first one had 5 breads and the second one 3. They thought, both can share 4 each. When they were about to eat, a third person came, asked them, if he could stay with them. They said ok,, since nobody could own that place. Since he had not brought any eatables with him, he requested them to give something to eat. They raised their doubt, how the available 8 breads could be shared between the three. The third person gave an idea – to cut each bread into 3 so that 5x3+3x3 = 24 pieces could be shared equally, with 8 for three. They did accordingly and they left for sleep comfortably. The next day morning, the third person started leaving. He not only thanked the other two, but also gave 8 gold coins, to be shared between them. After he had left, they started fighting with each other and claimed their share. The first one was claiming

"I gave more, so I should get more", second said "I had less, even then I gave mine for share." They could not come to a conclusion and they decided to go to the local Panchayat Chief.

The Chief, after hearing the case, expressed his inability and told them to wait for a day. He arranged for their stay. The verdict would be delivered on the next day. All gathered, to hear the verdict on the assigned time. The Chief said that the first person had 15 pieces to be shared and he got 8 pieces for his share to eat. The second had 9 pieces for sharing and he got 8. So what went, from the first for the third, were 7 and it was 1 from second. So the first should get 7, the second 1.

God is the right judge. HE will give what we deserve, not what we desire. Nothing more or less. It will be a razor edge precision.

The takeaway from this story is that, ***we may desire so many things, but we have to see, whether we are making ourselves deserving, to achieve those things. We have to equip ourselves, towards achieving our goals, in all our endeavours.***

The first requisite in that journey of achieving our ambitions is our passion.

Passion and Profession when go together, will make one do wonders – People who have passion in their profession have excelled and remain as a role model for others. Three examples for those people, are worth to be mentioned here.

First, a traffic constable in Chennai. Whether it is sun shine, or rain, he would be dancing and giving signal at the Chennai climate. When many are groaning, even about their cushy jobs, how this person can enjoy his monotonous job? It is obviously due to passion.

Second, an executioner, during second world war. He was carrying out the hanging of prisoners, that was only feeding him and his family. Even in that cruel and dirty job, he was following certain principles. He would see that that his prisoner should be killed, by the very first knot, so that the hanged need not undergo any torture, by not being killed by the first one and the need to repeat for the second time. What else, could be the reason for his act, other than passion even in that dirty and cruel job?

Third, a sculptor. He was making a statue. A visitor was passing by, who was noticing an exactly similar statue lying on the ground. He asked why this duplicate. The sculptor replied, that there was a scar in the nose of the statue, about which, he was not satisfied and so he was making another one. The visitor further questioned him, where that statue would be placed.'At the top of the temple tower', was the reply. The visitor then told him, in that case, nobody could notice the scar.

"No, No! My inner eyes would." quickly he remarked. This is the height of passion. When many present day employees, are having reckless care and indifferent attitude, towards their jobs, this sculptor is definitely a perfect role model

This type of passion will make one perform well in the assigned task and one requires that to excel in his career.

Passion with Efforts

While we talked about passion for performance, passion without efforts will pour only cold water. Read the following story concerning two stones:

Two stones were there at the outskirts of a village, upon which the villagers would be sitting, for time passing, doing their chit chat. Let us call the stones as YES and NO stones. One day, they heard a shocking news from such people, that a sculptor would be coming by next week, to select a stone, for making a Lord Vinayaka statue, to decorate the Vinayaka temple, coming up, in that village. Probably these two stones might also be the choice, they shared that information. While they were worried, if that be the case, where they would sit in future, for their time passing, the two stones started contemplating, about the torture they had to undergo, if those two would be selected for the purpose. The worry slowly turned into a panic. The NO stone firmly asserted, that it was not ready for the task. The YES stone said "if you are not ready, obviously the axe will fall on my neck only. No other go, I will be forced to accept, however unwilling I may be"

"No! No! Don't yield! You will have to undergo the worst torture. They will break you with a powerful machine. Cut mercilessly into pieces. Without any concern for your pain, they will scratch your body, with the emery paper, saying that they will polish you. Think twice and accept" NO stone tried to persuade the YES, for changing its mind.

"You may argue, so many things. We are like beggars. Beggars as you know, don't have any choice. I am forced to accept. Why we should cross the bridge before it comes? Let it come to reality. As of now, it is only a news." YES consoled itself.

That news became the reality, during the next week. The sculptor said, both the stones were perfectly matching for the job and he was much happy with those. Since NO stone was not ready for the task to be subjected, YES stone succumbed to the pressure.

NO stone was warning it. "See! the kind of torture, you are going to undergo will be very cruel. Change your mind" "No other go! Please leave me!" YES stone was moving reluctantly.

From next week onwards, the torturous sounds that reached the ears of NO stone made it shed tears. "How much pain and sorrow my friend is undergoing now?" It wept with pity. The 'victim' YES was having the feeling of killing pain, but soon became accustomed to it."I am glad that I am going to be the statue of Lord Vinayaka. That thought had tremendous soothing effect for YES

A few months passed. A cart was coming nearer to the NO stone". How are you?" a familiar voice was heard by NO stone. "Who are you?" asked NO stone."

"I am your friend YES. See, I have become the statue of Lord Vinayaka. If you want to see me, you have to join the queue at the temple. I am going to be installed as the statue there at the temple". The pity, NO stone had towards YES, thus far, had turned into a jealousy now." Why I did say no? Ought to have said yes like my friend" that type feeling was now, with NO It was further compounded, when the preparations were on, to have the colourful Kumbabishekam, a function at the temple to consecrate his friend, as the presiding deity. It felt heavily for the mistake committed. It was full of woes. Its agony went to the peak, when some of the priests who came for the function, chose it, for breaking open the coconuts to be offered to the Lord. One, tens, hundreds and thousands of coconuts were broken on its head. While his friend YES, was ready to undergo a temporary pain for the bigger gains to be adorned as the Lord statue, his reluctance to that has made it suffer endlessly. While it was afraid of the temporary pain, with the task of being converted into a statue, it had to be accustomed to the permanent pain, with the innumerable coconuts, broken on its head - present, future and for ever. What is the use of crying over spilt milk? It was haunted with self pity. YES stone in the form of Lord Vinayaka, was giving dharshan, to all the devotees, coming in queue. NO stone, was undergoing the minute by minute torture, of coconut-breaking by the countless devotees. A mutually difference, in their paradigm shift, with respect to their attitude, made a huge difference in their life - one with perfect dividends, the other with perpetual pains.

The take away from this story is **No Pain No Gain**, Melted metal alone can become a vessel. Heated gold, will only become an ornament. Broken and polished stone can only turn into a statue.

Whether working for the owner, or be an entrepreneur, we should keep this in mind. Success or monetary benefits won't come in search of us. We have to toil for those.

TV Sundaram Iyengar, the noted and eminent Industrialist, started the iconic TVS group in Tamilnadu. During the initial stages of starting his automobile workshop in South, he brought his two young sons and introduced them to the manager in the shop. He said "these are two are your management trainees, treat them as the trainees. The thought, that they are your owner's son should never come to your mind. They should work hard to learn all jobs." One of the secrets of TVS's success lies in these types of approaches. During those periods, when TVS road transport buses were plying on the road, people would use to see their arrival time and try to set the time in their watch or clock. Such was their brand image.

This type of brand image, in fact stems from the individual, who matters more, in any organisation. That self image of that individual, irrespective of the field, he or she is in, should be high.

A TV anchor once asked Martina Navratilova, a renowned tennis player "How do you maintain your focus and manage to keep playing, even at the age of 43?"

Her suave response was, "The ball doesn't know, how old I am.' Such was her self image, which transformed into a powerful brand image, for her.

In his excellent book, ***Still Power***, Sports Psychologist Garret Kramer says that, a key factor to performing well in sports (and in life), is your ability to control the quality and quantity of your "internal dialogue". It can be given as an equation,

Performance = Potential – Internal Interference

In other words, you need to stop yourself from stopping yourself. Our internal interferences, in terms of negative outlook, obsessions, lethargic attitude, postponing etc will affect our performance.

Sports, fitness, business and indeed Life are played on a 6-inch ground ...the space between our own two ears! Our head, in between the two ears takes many crucial decisions. Let it think positively and the performance be enhanced.

Which Type You are?

Our nation requires more of these SR Types now, to enable India, to become a super power in the world.

Old Song! Novel Lessons!

Oru kudam thanni vittu oru poo pooththathu irandu kudam thanni vittu irandu poo poothththathu........................

Many in Tamil Nadu would not have missed this song in our elementary school. It is meant for teaching basic mathematical table through vaippaadu, as they call in Tamil. If we pour one **kudam** meaning one pot of water, we will get one **poo** or one flower, two pots will give two flowers and so on. The level of truth behind the above song was confined only, to pot and flower for an elementary school level student. If we go deeper, we will get the clarity, that the pot here represents effort and flower the result. The central idea in this song, can be summarized in one simple sentence. Pots and flowers are directly proportional. It can be extended further, that efforts and results are directly proportional. With further probing into the pots and flowers analogy itself, we will get more insights. Can we get convinced with the fact, that the efforts and results are directly proportional, in all the cases, with all the people at all times? The answer will be a firm **NO!**

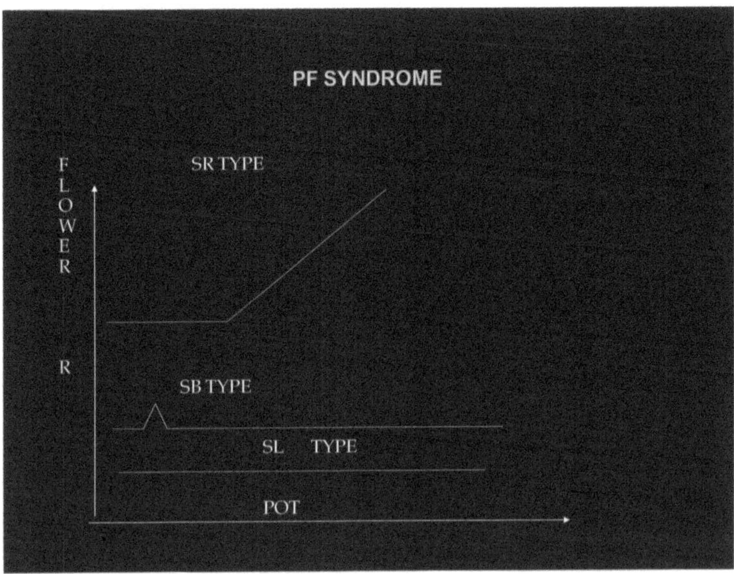

My own research with many people, has derived some interesting facts, based on the above concept The study is graphically depicted as above, under the caption, POT-FLOWER, or PF Syndrome. With some people – let them be called as **Category I** for the time being – they will be contented and happy with the flowers they get, for the pots they pour. They won't pour more pots, so as to get more flowers. With some – let them be called as **Category II** – they will have a fantastic initial start, with bubbling interest and enthusiasm. But the pity is, that their interest will dwindle or be completely flat, after a specified period of time. Some-let them be called as **Category III** – will not get any flowers even after say 50 pots. They won't be dejected and will continue to pour more pots. To their surprise and joy, one flour will start coming after say, the 51st pot. At the 52nd pot, not two flowers, but say 20 flowers will blossom. After this period, which I call it, as the break point, they will plenty of flowers, not in linear proportions but in geometric measures. Their persistence, on the set goals, to get flowers and their patience and perseverance, to wait for the flowers to blossom, will pay dividends. As it is said, noth ing succeeds like success, it is no wonder, that they will be able to get sustained results. It is also equally important, that they will be able to maintain the momentum throughout, without any complacency, after tasting the initial success. They are neither fed up with failures, nor over-confident with success.

SL Type

The category I mentioned above, is named by me, as **SL Type** or **Straight Lined type** of people, who are contented with the results, they get for the efforts, they put in at the specified period of time. Even though, they can make further efforts, they won't. They are unwilling to come out of their comfort zone.

To quote an example, a youth who was taking rest by the side of a pond, in a village at 11 o' clock in the morning, was awakened by an old man. "Don't you have any job?" for this question from the old man he replied "my daily job would be over at 9 o' clock itself". He went on further, saying that his job would be to get fifty fish from the pond, which he would hand over to his wife She would sell the harvested fish at the nearby market. Part of the money would be given to him. He would have liquor and take rest, as he was doing then. The caring old man, on inspecting the fishing net, found it very dirty and worn out. He hastened the youth to come along with him, to a bank in the same village, to get a loan for buying a new net. To his query, "What is the necessity for a new net now?" the youth was answered, by the old man, with the new net, he would get not 50 fish, but much more in the same pond and he could repay the loan quickly and buy few more nets. ....the dialogue was continuing, with the old man's saying that he could buy a boat, employ more people and take rest. The youth retorted "that is what lam doing it now? Why the trouble of getting a new net, more fish, still more nets and boat ....so on and so forth?". The disgusted old man left with a broken heart. These kinds of people cannot be changed. The youth here is an example of SL type. Even though he has the physical strength and capabilities of earning more, he is not willing to do so. There are ample examples of this SL type. In this cut throat competitive world, marked by intense competition and uncertainty, many think that the present conditions will hold good for the future too, which is contrary to the reality. They are unwilling to come out of their comfort zone and they will surely be the victims, to the harsh reality, marked by many unforeseen and uncertain situations. They will not even pay heed to the advice given by their well wishers (as is the case with the youth, mentioned above, who was averse, to the advice by the old man). These SL type people can't cope up with the present day world. They are completely forgetting, that they have to struggle now in order not to struggle in future.

SB Type

The category II type is named by me, as the **SB Type or Soda Bottle Type** people. The soda bottle when opened, will bubble with effervescence initially, but it will subside quickly. The momentum will not last long. These SB Type people will start many new tasks with much initial enthusiasm. That will not be sustained. A youth longing to maintain good health and pursuing yoga classes, but doing it only for a week and thereafter stopping to do, a lady wanting to reduce her weight by strict diet system, discontinuing it after a week with many lame excuses, an employee wanting to pursue the part time BE course, stopping after the first semester – examples like these can be multiplied. These type of people in families or organisations or in societies, are highly unreliable, who can't be given any new responsibilities. They will not be able to pursue their goal vigorously. Their chances of coming up in life will be very less.

SR Type

The category III is named by me, as the **SR type or Sustained Result type**. They will be bubbling with enthusiasm throughout. They will not be depressed by the initial set backs, they will have enormous will power and inner strength to pursue and complete the assigned tasks. Obstacles or difficulties will not mar their interest. Success will not go to their head nor failure to their heart. They will learn from failures, consider it, as the stepping stones for success.

Some of the prominent Individuals who can be grouped under the above category are:-

Amitabh Bachchan, Elvis Presley, Wilma Rudolph, Ramakrishnan of Amar Seva Sagam

In the organisational field, the following corporates are some of the examples:-

Crompton Greaves, Whirlpool, Eicher, Indigo Airlines, Spicejet, India Cements, Royal Enfield, Indian Rayon

It has been found, that the following qualities, are possessed by the above category:-

1. **Control of Situations:-**

   They won't allow the situations, to sit on their head. They will not be bowed down by the threats. They will boldly face the threats or even convert the threats, into their opportunities. To quote some classic examples:-

   a. In the late sixties, all the Japanese goods were dumped in US, for which the latter wanted to put an entry barrier. The Government arranged to display many posters, with the message of asking the people 3to stay off Japanese goods. Since printing technology was not that much developed in US, at that time, they employed many artists, who were in the process of making manual posters. About this, one article appeared in a business journal long back. It would go like this:

      An American artist will be making a poster, with the caption – **US wants you to say off Japanese goods**! A Japanese executive, with a small brief case, in his hand with the word written – **yenterprises** (as against the usual spelling of" **enterprises"** – he had – **yenterprises** – starting with the name of their currency, yen – depicting their patriotism) would enter and ask the artist,

      "Why are you wasting your precious time? Buy this printing machine!. Print any number of posters you want!"

The threat to their products, is very cleverly converted in to an opportunity of buying yet another new product. The Japanese are experts in converting the situation to their advantage, however challenging it may be.

b. IBM was the first to introduce Computers. Apple was the first to give PC. Bowed down by the threat from apple, IBM also started to manufacture PCs. Sensing the threat from the giant, IBM , Apple released a paper ad saying

'Welcome IBM , welcome to our field'

It was a very subtle and shrewd message to IBM – 'after all you imitated our product and we are the first in giving PC.'

SR Type persons or organisations will possess this characteristic to maintain their position in the cut-throat competitive world.

2. **Practical Intelligence**:-

To quote an anecdote, again with the Japanese/American example:

Two employees – one from US and another from Japan, were working for an MNC, situated at the bottom of a hill. Every morning, they used to go for jogging. One day when the American was ready, the Japanese was tightening his shoe lace. Being urged for the quick start, the Japanese had a non verbal communication-pointing his thumb finger at the back. To his utter shock, the American noticed a threatening tiger. The American somehow managed and posed the question- "Just because you are tightening your shoe lace, do you think that you can run faster than this ferocious tiger?"

The Japanese at once replied" No! It is not my aim, to run faster than this tiger, but to run faster than you."

That message conveyed is with practical intelligence – ***what is the right, desired act to be pursued at the need of the hour with utmost shrewdness.*** The tiger was going to aim any one of them. "Why I should be the victim?" That was the thought process, which was going on, in the mind of that Japanese. In fact these kinds of approaches in the volatile business world, enabled Japanese, in sustaining their positions. In the competitive world, the motto' I should be the winner' will be with this SR type, the fire in their belly, will never be off.

3. **Asking the right type of questions**:-

SR type will not search for right answer, instead they will ask the right type of questions. 'What is my strength and weakness, with respect to my approach towards the pursued goal, what are the opportunities and threats-coupled with this SWOT (Strength, weakness, opportunities, threats) analysis, they will wait for the right moment and hit the target. An anecdote, though a negative example drives home this point.

An alchemist (a person in the process of converting iron into gold) was getting only 80% success in his attempts. Unable to proceed further on his own, he approached his friend and a well wisher, for expert guidance. As per his directions, he reached the top of Himalayas where the concerned person with the right formula for 100 % conversion was supposed to be residing. He was also keeping in mind, about the warning from his friend, that he should restrict the question to only one, since the expert at the Himalayas, would not answer more than one question. Amidst all the hurdles and difficulties, he reached the desired location. Knocking at the door, he was waiting for the person to open. The door was opened from inside. To the surprise of the alchemist, that person was a beautiful lady. Completely awe-struck, at the intoxicating beauty of the lady, forgetting the purpose for which he came, he asked the question-"Are you married?" "No"! The lady went inside. It would be anybody's guess, what would have been the net result of his mission. The focus of the alchemist was not clear. The primary focus was pushed into background. Ambitions should always be accompanied by the right approach. That can be possible only, if one asks the right type of questions. Deviations from the primary goal should never occupy one's mind.

Contrary to the alchemist's stand, the SR type will ask the right type of questions, instead of searching for the right answers. Right questions beget the right answers. That is the hallmark of the success of SR type. Individuals or organizations who are able to sustain their positions amidst the fierce competitions possess this quality.

4. **Going beyond the conventional wisdom**:-

This is yet another quality that SR type possesses. They won't confine themselves to the normal boundaries. They go far beyond that. They will not only practice that but will also encourage those pursuing that.

Yet another Japanese example. A particular company was manufacturing soap. Soap, instead of being given, in conventional wrappers, was given in a box. It was not, that the customers would get a soap box free. The product was the brain child of the Chief Executive. To the shock of the C. E., one customer got a soap box without soap, which was directly reported to him. Terribly annoyed, he called all the senior executives, asked them to find out a suitable method to detect this fault so that this mistake would not get repeated. When he was almost trying to implement one of the suggested methods-installing an automated, relatively cost effective software with a scanner, which will identify the empty soap box, if any, and automatically discarding it and another method, with the automated software having a weighing machine, detecting the empty soap box and so on – one lower level employee came to his cabin and he gave a suggestion, of installing a high speed pedestal fan, at the conveyor belt, in which the final products were moving for dispatch. It would automatically throw off the empty soap box. The whole process was changed and this very cheap method was implemented. The person, who was thinking laterally or creatively or beyond the boundaries-whatever name we could give – was rewarded. Japanese are creative and they encourage creativity. That is why they are able to give sustained results in spite of the severe set backs, they come across in their native land due to the natural calamities.

SR Type, besides going beyond conventional wisdom, encourages those possessing it, which is one of the secrets of their success. Not only that. They value their customer complaints. They consider the complaints as chances for making improvements in their processes.

Above all, the unifying threads, that pervade through all the above qualities, are the 3Ps – **Persistence, Perseverance and Patience** which make them deliver sustained results, amidst all the threats. ***Our nation requires more of these SR Types now, to enable India, to become a super power in the world.***

While these are the very positive lessons to be learnt there are negative ones as well:

There was a bachelor wood cutter in a village. Very pious he was, would go to temple daily, pray to God in the village temple, before starting to the forest for his job. One day, when he was taking rest, he saw a fox crawling with two legs. Shortly after, he saw a tiger dragging a dead deer, ate some portions and left the remaining, which were consumed by the handicapped fox. The fox happily ate the portions and stayed happily. These kinds of acts, he could notice several times. He inferred the message, that God would give the feed to the needy. He prayed for that kind of boon, remained lazy and idle, without doing any work. Days passed. He was fed up with God, that he did not arrange any food, as done for the fox. He became very weak as well. Very angirily, he shouted at God, that HE deceived him mercilessly. God answered him through HIS voice" you fool! I showed the example of fox and tiger to you, with the message,' I will feed the underprivileged like fox, through the good samaritans like the tiger. You should have taken the tiger, as your role model. Unfortunately you took the wrong example of fox. That is your mistake'

The message through this story is – ***God is not our servant to work for us. HE will only work with us. you. Manushaprayathnam and Deiva Sankalpam (efforts by human beings and the God's grace) will alone bring the results. Let us continue our work, earn more, help the needy people.***

Classification from Scriptures:-

While we have seen the examples of 3 types of persons, through the POT-FLOWER example, scriptures give examples of three more types. They are:-

1. **Gajakarnam** – these are like the elephant, which will not rest at a specific place, but will wander here and there. Like the elephant, these people will not stick to a specific task, but switch over to multiple tasks, without fulfilling their goals.
2. **Ajakarnam** – these are like a goat. A goat, if touched on its tail, will lower its head. These type of people, when pointed out with their mistake will not accept the same and resort to self defence.
3. **Gokarnam** – These are like a cow. Whichever part of a cow one touches, its whole body will get excited. These type of people will be responsive to the criticism, pointed out by others and correct themselves.

For success in practical life, one has to be a 'Gokarnam Type'

Shoe Adjusting to Leg

Another caution for the youngsters, while joining an organisation is that they have to match themselves to the culture of the organisation, not the vice versa. The leg need not adjust to the shoe, but the shoe should.

In whichever aspect one is strong he should choose that kind of job which will enable him to put his best. A sales person was advised by his supervisor that customer would always be the boss. He could not get convinced on this and argued that they could be also wrong sometimes. He resigned his job one day, joined as a police constable, where he was expected to see others with suspicion and his diction, customer can also be wrong was becoming true. He shined well as a constable. The point is, one should choose a job, fitting to his attitude and interests. If he is not happy with the job or the organisation, it is better to leave the organisation, without groaning or cursing the organisation. Live to the culture or leave the organisation – should be the policy

How to avoid frustration in an organization – apt advice by a professional:

A training programme was being conducted, by a renowned resource person. After his inputs, one of the participants, working in a top MNC raised his queries during the question answer session.

"I joined an MNC as a trainee and after 30 years of my service, I have become one of the vice presidents with the same MNC. I had very high interest and enthusiasm initially, which I find slowly waning. With the family – the same family, with the same caring wife (telling with a smile) and two loving children – my interest and involvement, never dwindle out. Why sir, why? Can you clarify?"

Without answering his question directly, the resource person, instead asked him,

"Who prepares food, for you at home? Your wife or your mother?"

"My wife" came the answer.

"Will you say your wife cooks the food or serves the food?"

"Cooking is secondary. Even a paid cook can prepare the food. But my wife serves the food with care which is more significant."

"Exactly. Anybody can cook the food. But serving with care and concern, can only be done, by the affectionate person-be it wife or mother. She works in the kitchen which is secondary but she happily serves you, that is primary. You like her food not just for her cooking, but all the more for her careful serving. She enjoys her serving to the family members. She does not get any remuneration for the act which is great." continuing his argument, the resource person went on further saying-

"Why can't we apply this concept to our work situation? Why should we say that I am working for this X organisation. Why can't we say that we are serving this organisation. Instead of saying, I am working for this organisation and getting a salary, why can't we say Iam serving for this organisation and I am paid service charges for the service rendered for the organisation. If we have this paradigm shift in our outlook, we can be happy in whatever job, we are doing. The Vice president got convinced.

It is an eye opener for many. When we see many employees, looking down upon their job and with a grudge towards their boss or organisation, this kind of change in attitude will be of paramount importance, to both the individuals and their organisation.

Ishtam not Kashtam

Do your job with Ishtam (liking) but not with kashtam (difficulty). Job done with Ishtam will not be stressful, instead, it will be joyful. An anecdote comes to my mind, at this context.

An unmarried youth was asked by his aged mother to replace the empty gas cylinder in the kitchen, from another room, with a fresh one.

"No! no! How can I? very heavy."

The aged mother was murmuring, "Last week I saw you lifting your girl friend at the beach. You did not mind about her bulky body. But this cylinder seemed to be heavy for you."

The poor mother does not realise that lifting a sixty kg girl friend, is easier for his son, because he does it with ishtam. Lifting a sixteen kg cylinder is apparently felt heavier, because he is doing that with kashtam. All because of our attitude towards, whatever we do.

Any job done with ishatam will not be painful but pleasant. This paradigm shift in our outlook will make us execute the job effectively.

Success Stories from Achievers

So, if you ever think, it's too late to be successful, just remember John B. Goodenough. Age is not a bar for new inventions: he is a very good role model in that direction.

We have heard the success stories of so many achievers, whose life lessons, are inspirations for us. One such is from a person, who struggled with ordeals, with ultimate success, is given below:-

From Travel Industry:-

Hailing from a very downtrodden family, from the south of Tamilnadu, he could not continue beyond 8th standard. His ancestors were doing the slavery job. Unwilling to do that type of job, he left for Chennai, at his late twenties. No experience and no knowledge of any job.

Did not know anybody in the city. Platform was his dwelling place. While searching for a job, in the hotels or travel agencies, he was driven out, He was informed, that without anybody's recommendation, no job would be given.

He was staying and sleeping with beggars and leppers. On one such night, policemen were driving out those people, which will be a routine for them. Being afraid of being caught and put behind the bars, he ran fast and the policeman chasing him, could not run. He stopped at a place near Annasalai in Chennai, where some people were sleeping. To choose a very safe place, he joined with them. To his surprise, next day morning, one person woke him up and asked him" hello! Can you spare this seat? I will give money." He was puzzled. Again he asked' how much you want '?He said two rupees. Then only he stared at that place. It was American Embassy Branch at Anna salai, Chennai. At that period, those who were going to get the US visa, would try to get a seat in the queue and will have this arrangement. The first income he got was that two rupee, with which he had a good food on that day. Knowing the trick of the game, he plunged into the business and started earning more. He got into the contacts of travel agents and started doing commission business for them. He was very loyal to the agents and the customers. His hard work and dedication earned a good reputation for him

One incident he could not forget in his life. He was to hand over the passport and ticket to the travelers going by ship from Rameswaram to Srilanka. The train, by which he travelled stopped at Mandapam station. He was told that the train would not go further. Unless those documents were handed over to the ship passengers, they could not travel to Srilanka. It was 5AM on that day. He decided to walk through the train track and proceeded, via the black stones in between the track. After a while, he could not walk since there were no stones, but only the track. Below was the roaring sea, with a heavy wind. With courage and determination in his mind, he started crawling on the iron track and reached Pamban station, from where, got into a bus. It was 11am when he reached the designated ship, which was to start at 12 noon. The tense agents caught hold of the documents and did the formalities quickly. After a sigh of relief, he was surrounded by many agents and they heard the actual ordeals he underwent with awesome attention. That was the turning point for him. Soon he started his own travel agency called Madura travels at Mannadi, Chennai with a rented building for Rs 1500. Today he is a multi millionaire in his travel agency business. He is one of the authorized travel agencies by IATA and by all global embassies.

He is none other than V.K.T Balan of Madura travels, whose life lessons will be a true inspiration for youngsters. One cannot reach the success ladder easily. He will have to undergo many difficulties, trials and tribulations.

From Textile Industry:

How one can turn negatives into positives? Here is an awesome life story of K. R. Nagaraj the owner of Ramraj Cotton.

He was entering a five star hotel in Chennai along with his friends for a marriage reception function. All the other nine were allowed inside, except Nagaraj, the reason being, he was wearing a dhoti, which the hotel dress code won't permit. He took a vow on that day, that he would enter the same hotel, one day, with dhoti. He started a factory, producing men's wear including dhoti. He produced an ad film with the renowned actor Jayaram as the brand ambassador, the tile of the ad film being, SALUTE RAMRAJ. Whatever negatives he underwent, were shown as being converted into positives:

Ladies will press the gents to wear pants, instead of wearing dhoti, when the family goes out. In this ad the reverse – they will press for dhoti. College students will prefer only pants. Here they will prefer dhoti. The security at the five star hotel gate, will salute and greet the person with dhoti. Musicians will usually have more concentration on their concert. When a person with dhoti, enters the reception function, at a five star hotel, they will stop for a while and salute the person entering the hall. Elephants genrally don't like white colour, but in that ad film, it will garland the person with dhoti. For the business meet, all others will attend with formal dress. But the person with dhoti will be the chairman of the meet.

With profound proudness he used to say, that the same hotel which previosly disrespected him, for his dress code, did greet him with more respect, when he entered wearing dhoti after his success.

He is a perfect role model, as to how one person, can convert the threat into opportunities.

Is Age, a Bar to Excel?

At the age of 57, John B. Goodenough invented the lithium battery, which powers all our smart phones, tablets and laptops as well as electric cars.

37 years later at the age of 94, John has unveiled a new, ultra-efficient, low cost battery which uses a sodium or lithium coated glass electrolyte. It will dwarf his original invention and make it redundant.

The new glass battery will allow electric cars, to go three times the distance, and recharge in minutes instead of hours. It is also far safer, as it won't explode and can operate in sub-zero temperatures.

The new glass battery will power our future solar powered and electric vehicles, homes and industries.

But John isn't finished yet. He still works every day, as a Professor, at the University of Texas.

John believes, humanity has a 30 year window, to come up with an even more powerful 'super battery' to take us, entirely of fossil fuels, before the environmental damage, we are creating becomes irreversible, and he also says, "I want to solve this problem before my chips are in ... I still have time to go." What an inspiring confidence at that age?

So, if you ever think, it's too late to be successful, just remember John B. Goodenough. Age is not a bar for new inventions and he is a very good role model for that.

Wisdom on the Wheel

The world is a university. The beings you see, the people you come across, all are the valuable teachers for you. Keep your eyes, ears and minds open. You are sure to learn a lot

While the famous personalities, taught us distinct lessons, an ordinary cab driver taught me one day, in an extra ordinary way . . .

That day was altogether a different one for me. On that day I met a unique individual. What famous B – Schools could not teach, that cab driver, a simpleton, taught me. I still salute the person for his unusual wisdom. The name is immaterial. What we won't call a rose, may even smell sweet. The fragrance from his distilled wisdom, was filling my whole being, even after a month of my very short association, with him as his customer. Here goes my experience:

On my coming near the taxi, smartly dressed, with an attractive smile on his lips, that cab driver came around the car very enthusiastically to open the back door for me.

He handed me a laminated card and said 'I would like you to read my mission statement.'

Taken aback, I read the card. It said: ***To get my customers to their destination, in the quickest, safest and cheapest way possible, in a friendly environment and with a pleasurable experience.***

Each and every word had the truest sense of its integrity. Spotlessly clean taxi – inside and outside. A clean person with an unmistakable mind.

"Would you like a cup of coffee or tea?" I opted coffee and it was served hot.

He also handed over the daily newspapers and weekly magazines.

"Leave all these! Tell me, friend is this your regular practice with all the customers?"

"Yes and no! For the past three years, yes!. Before that, an honest no! I was complaining like all the rest of the cabbies do. Then I heard about POWER OF CHOICE one day." He continued further when I was curiously watching at his cute body language.

"Power of choice is, that you can be a duck, or an eagle. If you get up in the morning expecting to have a bad day, you will surely disappoint yourself. Stop complaining!"

"Don't be a duck. Be an eagle. Ducks quack and complain. Eagles soar above the crowd.

I decided to change my attitude and become an eagle. I looked around at the other cabs and their drivers. The cabs were dirty, the drivers were unfriendly, and the customers were unhappy. So I decided to make some changes, slowly …a few at a time. When my customers responded well, I did more.".

I could not turn my eyes back from that unusual driver. "Anything more to share, my dear friend?" I persuaded him for more.

"God made me the owner of this taxi after 5 years of my hard work. Two more taxis are running for two different cab operators. You people would advise, for putting eggs in different baskets.

Anything may happen at any time We should be proactive". Putting eggs, proactive – these words were coming out of an ordinary driver. He seemed to be different.

He continued. "I hail from a very poor family. Born into a poor family was my fate. If I die in the same state, that will be my own blunder". He made me sit at the edge of my seat.

"Not able to continue after plus 2 , I joined as a cleaner under a lorry driver. Slowly learnt the tricks of the trade and got the statutory driving license. After fifteen years of toiling, with many ups and downs, now I am the owner of three taxis. Each and every part of those three vehicles, will speak of my sweat and toil." wiping his face with a spotlessly white handkerchief, he added "I learnt many valuable lessons from this driving job sir. Will you be interested to listen?"

"Why not? With pleasure! please go ahead!" My body language, was that of an elementary school student, listening stories from his grandma. My ears, mind and the soul were all in complete readiness to absorb the teachings. Words of wisdom were flowing in full spontaneity from that ordinary person with an entirely different outlook.

All those, that came from him, were very sincerely decoded by me later. He shared his valuable experiences and the lessons learnt, as a driver, which can be aptly rephrased, as the learning for anybody, starting his or her career For the sake of convenience and clarity, his statements have been given under 'His', followed by my decoding, under 'Mine', which should be the take away for freshers, from the colleges, for a brighter career. Here they are:

His:- *I realised that getting a driving license, does not make me a driver. I got my license at my 18th age. But I could become a reasonably good driver, only after several months of continuous practice.*

Mine:- After getting a degree or diploma, many students think that they have achieved something unique. A driving license is only a permit and not a stamp of authority. Likewise a MBA or any degree does not qualify one, to be a manager, or for that matter, a BE degree does not qualify oneself to be an engineer. After several years of dedicated service, coupled with continuous learning, one can become a reasonably good manager or an efficient engineer. Getting a degree is only a beginning and it is not an end for learning. Continuous updating of knowledge, suited to the market dynamics, is all needed. The license of getting a degree or a diploma makes one as qualified, for learning from the real life experiences, suitably matching the both. The concepts learnt, are not that much significant, but relating those principles, to the real organizational life, will alone make a real manager. Getting a license somehow, will not guarantee for being a good driver. Skillful driving of a car, at a terrific traffic, can alone speak of an effective driver. Mugging up the concepts and vomiting at the examination hall, may enable a student to score good marks. But that does not help anyway in the real life, which is totally a different environment altogether.

His:- *After getting a license I learnt to drive a car. The first vehicle given to me for driving, was different from the one, with which I practiced my learning. The various parts like gears steering wheel etc all were totally different. Even though, I claimed that I got driving license, I could not even start quickly, the first vehicle assigned to me initially.*

Mine:- The classroom learning is totally secured, The real business world is cut throat and highly demanding. The engineers, who learnt the subjects in the class room, see a completely different world, when they enter into the organisational set up. This is applicable for CAs/ICWAs or ACSs or MBAs etc. They should be equipped, to face the real practical world which requires to develop tremendous skill, patience and will power. Case studies taught in B-schools can help one, to acquire the analytical and problem solving skills. But the problems encountered, in the actual corporate world are entirely different. That require much more home work – meshing the theory and practice with acquired experiences, unlearning, learning and relearning, made in each situation.

His:- *I realised the most valuable lesson – No pain no gain. I was ready to make my hands dirty. There were many occasions, where I learnt a* *lot, by working as a cleaner, that enabled me to peep and learn about the inner parts of a car. That clearly paved the way, for my becoming a good driver. What I learned beneath the bonnet, did go a long way in my career*

Mine: If we ask the successful marketing professionals about the secrets of their achievements, they will all uniformly say, that the practical lessons they learnt, are from their experiences in petty shops scattered in lanes. Convincing the small shop owner, requires tremendous persuasion skills and herculean efforts, which can't be taught in B-schools. The ground realities are different from the marketing concepts, taught to them and they need to apply multifarious techniques to sell their products. Marketing without sales is nothing. When many fresh graduates opt for customer relations job,(read – they want A/C room jobs) they conveniently forget that their learning becomes highly limited. One should not mind in working harder, dirtying the dress There is no other easier way, in this cut throat competitive world to come up in life.

His:- *In the early years, what you learn, is more important, than what you earn. In spite of my owner being very nice, the salary was very meager in my first job,. But he gave me more freedom. I had more opportunities to learn by the mistakes made. He tolerated my mistakes and reposed enormous trust on me. That gave me a nice atmosphere, to work with and it boosted my morale.*

Mine:- More than the salary, joining a good organisation with a good boss, as a mentor is all more important in anybody's career. That will lay a good foundation for their future prospects. That will be a priceless boon. Pay pocket is secondary. A good boss and the right working environment can compensate other shortcomings.

His:- *Don't worry about which car you drive. Focus on being a good driver. I won't have any specific preferences for the models of the cars. I won't say that I will drive only the best cars, I won't be interested to drive public transport, school van or tempo etc. My focus was on driving well. The type of vehicles, was not a matter of concern for me. But, how well I drive the assigned vehicle, is all the more important. Getting* *acquainted with different models of the car, will expose me to a variety of experiences and the associated learning*

Mine:- Now that is a great lesson. It is not about the organisation. It is about the individual. Don't have any preferences or any prejudices. Focus on your learning curve. No job is inferior. Excel in each job assigned. Contribute your best to the organisation. The rewards will come sooner or later. Sometimes the rewards may come very late, but it will come with compound interest.

Instead of job hopping, stay focused on giving the best, to all the assigned jobs. Develop a personal mission statement and stick to that. Be an eagle not a duck. Success, happiness and of course, the money will automatically come. Excel in each job assigned. Please don't forget – ***Every job is the self portrait of the person who did it. Autograph your work with excellence.***

That day was full of pleasurable and memorable experience for me. He taught this HR Faculty very valuable lessons. I was totally absorbed in his informal talk. ***It was as if I was like 'Arjuna' before that 'Krishna'.***

Looking Around:-

The world is a university – each and every being created by HIM is teaching some lessons or other. How?

While we are studying under a teacher, he or she teaches lessons first, then only asks us to undergo the test. The GOD ALMIGHTY is altogether a very different and hard teacher. HE puts us under test first and expects us to learn lessons from that. What lessons we learn and whether we are applying those lessons to correct us – all these will tell about the success or failure in our life.

It is not that, HE expects us to learn from the fellow human beings, sometimes even from the animals or any creatures, under his creation.

We all know of Amoeba, that single cell creature. That single cell symbolizes individuality or rigidity – under any circumstances, one should never give up his 'being'. If we fall for everything, we stand for nothing. That single cell creature, teaches this moral. The same amoeba will take varied shapes, suited to different situations. These 'varied shapes' denote flexibility – one should be flexible in his approach, for maintaining a harmonious relationship. In terms of ideals or principles, one should be like a rock – be very rigid. In terms of relationship, one should be like a river-be flexible.

So, not only amoeba, the rock and the river too teach us very valuable lessons. Where all, we should be rigid, and where all, we should be flexible, are determined by circumstances or situations. We should only keep our ears, eyes and minds open, to get the right cues.

Take the case of a mosquito. We all know that the mosquitoes bite us and suck our blood. But how many of us, know that only female mosquitoes bite? That too, it won't bite the pregnant ladies. When many money lenders, are sucking the blood of innocent poor, through exorbitant interest, isn't this tiny creature teaching us the valuable lessons of ethics and values to be learnt from them?

Look at the ants. A small piece of jaggery or a drop of honey, when spilled on a floor, hundreds of ants will immediately rush there to collect their food. Imagine a huge collection of assorted sweets, kept in a jar, being surrounded by a plate, containing water. Will the ants go nearer? Never! No doubt, it is in search of its much needed food for survival. But, at the same time, it analyses the pros and cons – the distinct possibilities of the harsh reality. The food for its survival or its very survival of its own life? It does not take even an inch of risk. It goes away from the "food". Aren't we able to learn the most valuable lessons – SWOT analysis as we call in management-strength, weakness, opportunities and threats? Or Look before you Leap-kind of lessons? Ponder over that.

In the same token, the very ant, with all its difficulties, carries a leaf much bigger than its own size, as its food and tries to take forward to its dwelling place, a tiny hole, at the corner of the wall, in that room. Upon realising that, it cannot take that big leaf through that tiny hole, it simply drops the leaf and proceeds alone into the hole. It carries out a clear analysis of the situations and the circumstances and takes the most right decision. While we are able to appreciate the presence of God Almighty in, as its brain, we are also able to make out the most valuable life lessons, learnt from this tiny creature.

A lesson taught by a saint is worth quoted here. A saint was asked to rate the rule of his king. He, at once replied – 'Cat's teeth'. The person who questioned him, was not able to understand and asked the saint to explain further. The saint went on to say "While catching its prey, the rat, its teeth would become merciless. It would tear the rat into pieces. No pity, no compassion. The same teeth, while carrying its kitten, will be very soft, to the younger one, without giving even an inch of pain. See! the same teeth! How different are the two approaches, how it can be at the two extremes? What do you learn from this?". To this question by the saint, the person replied" the king will be merciless towards the enemies and at the same time, he will be very kind and compassionate towards his own people." "Alright, there is something more than this. Looking from an another perspective-if you ask the opinion of the cat's teeth, with a rat, what answer will it give? Very treacherous, very cruel isn't it? If the same question is posed to a kitten, the answer will be totally different. Very soft, cushion like. Is it not? So, the cat's teeth, when viewed from two different entities, the responses are, in fact, falling into the two different extremes. If we like a person, our opinions about that person, will be very positive. If we don't, the words about that person will become totally negative. We operate from these biased attitude. If we want to have the right picture, about a being or a person in this world, we should be free from bias or prejudices. We should be objective in our approach." the saint concluded his revelations. A simple cat's teeth teaches us, this precious lesson.

A famous Guruji was in his death bed. Surrounding him, his disciples asked him, who was his favourite Guru. He said feebly "Hundreds! How can I pin point any?" The followers pressed him to mention a few. The Guruji replied" alright I will name only three! "The first one was a thief!"

"Thief" wondered the disciples. Guruji continued" yes! once I was passing through a small town and searching for a place to stay for a month. A person offered, to take me to his house and after reaching the place only, I leant to know that he was a thief, staying alone in that house. Every day he would go for theft, but would return only empty-handed. But he would be very optimistic and would say daily "I would get something tomorrow". One month passed, without any return for him. He was very optimistic. Tomorrow I would get. He would rather tell me "Please pray for me sincerely so that I would get at least tomorrow" I was overwhelmed with his high degree of optimism. I also learnt persistence in his goal, patience in his mind and perseverance in his efforts. He was one of my most revered Gurujis.

"Who is the second?" for the query he replied "a dog! When I was going to take bath in a river once, I saw a dog that was trying to drink water from the river, standing from its bank. When it saw its own image, reflected in the river water, it assumed it to be an another dog, as a rival. It was going on barking at its' rival 'and the reflection repeated the same act. It never gave up. Finally it jumped in to the river water and drank to its satisfaction. It was surprised to know there is nothing, called its 'rival'. I learnt the most valuable lesson form that dog-most of our fears are unfounded, all illusory. When we dare those, they would automatically vanish. My second guru, that dog, taught this precious lesson.

"The third Guru was a small child. I saw him lighting a lamp with a source of fire. I asked him "You have lighted the lamp from that source. where did the fire come from?". I posed myself as the most intelligent, and the poor little boy, I assumed would not be able to answer that question. The little child put off the lamp, with the blowing of air from his mouth, and he in turn asked the question to me "where this fire has gone?". Without waiting for the answer from me, he simply ran away. I was thinking, I knew everything. But that little child shattered my ego. He was my greatest Guru.

Dear disciples! Don't even underestimate anybody. The world is a university. The beings you see, the people you come across, all are the valuable teachers for you. Keep your eyes, ears and minds open. You are sure to learn a lot

Let this advice be a beacon, to guide us, in all our endeavours

Attitude Will Take to Altitude

Unspent money devalues, idle machinery disintegrates, unutilized time dies, so also the unused potential

A Little boy went to a telephone booth, which was at the cash counter of a shop: he dialed a number. The shop-owner observed and listened to the conversation:

Boy: Sir, can I get a job to work in your lawn?

Other end: I have already one

Boy: Sir, I will work at half of the salary, you pay now.

Other end: Sorry, Iam getting a very satisfied work from the present person

Boy: Sir, I can give free service at your staircase

Other end: Please excuse me. I am not willing to relieve that person

With a smile on his face, the little boy put the receiver down.

The shop-owner, who was listening to all this, came to the boy.

Shop-owner: I am ready to offer job, if you are ready. I have a vacancy in my house

Boy: Sorry to decline your precious offer

Shop-owner: I heard that you were virtually begging for that job.

Boy: I was in fact trying to make out from my present employer about my performance, in an indirect way. Yes, he is my present boss.

The small boy taught us very big lessons. This is called "Self-Appraisal" Nobody can be a best judge, other than the self, regarding one's job. Do your best. Automatically rewards or recognitions will come.

Give your best and the world will come to you!

Don't relax or show laziness. Younger generations should ponder over this in their mind.

A famous quote said by Lord Krishna in Bhagvat Gita, is apt to be mentioned here:

"If You don't fight for what you want, don't cry for what you lost…"

"Nothing depends on luck, everything depends on work, because, even luck has to work."

Useful Insights from Sukha, Son of Ved Vyasa:-

The sage Ved Vyasa wanted his son, to get supreme knowledge. To King Janaka, Sukha was sent. Sukha went to enter, King's palace. Sukha was not allowed by the servants. For seven days, entry was refused. On the 8th day, into palace, he was taken by Janaka himself in a big procession. Sukha was given the best hospitality for seven days, but he was not attracted by any. Next day, he was given an open vessel, filled to brim with oil, he was asked to go round a big hall, seven times and to ensure oil did not spill. On his way, many distractions were there, like drum beatings, music, dance. Sukha concentrated only on the work assigned, without being distracted. A servant came and inserted a sugar candy. When the servant returned after some time, to his surprise it was not wet, not melting or being swallowed. King Janaka was extremely happy to hear this.

He embraced him saying "My son, you achieved your goal. Without being attracted by the luxuries, your sole aim was on the purpose, for which, you came. This is the supreme knowledge, I want you to gain. I am glad that you acquired that. No more to learn further.

Suga teaches us a very valuable lesson

Goal concentration, despite all the distractions, will fetch the desired results.

Very Positive Lessons from a Negative Situation:-

We have had more insights from very renowned personalities. Why not from the negatives?

Two robbers were planning to rob a rich man's house. They had a spy, who was a servant, working in that bungalow. For the bribe, he got from them, he disclosed all the vital information-where the costly things had been kept, how to enter that particular room etc etc. The problem for the robbers was, as to how to get into that room. There was a big neem tree, rooted at a place outside the compound wall. It had a lengthy branch, say hundred metres, which started outside the compound wall and went very nearer to the room, where the costly things had been kept. There was no other way, by which they could approach the room. If they could walk confidently through that branch, the job would have almost been over, following the instructions given by their bribed spy. They had the will to walk through the lengthy branch, but not the skill. They are not experienced in that task. For carrying out any task, for that matter, one requires both the skill and will. The robbers were clearly lacking the skill. They were in a fix. They didn't want to lose the big chunk of that treasure. Their minds were thinking seriously. If they could get a skilled person, to walk through the branch, task can be finished with the further instructions, given from their side to the assigned person.

They went around the city, on the look out for a suitable person. To their luck, they spotted a gypsy who could definitely be the right fit. Walking through that branch would obviously be a child's play for him. But the gypsy was initially not having the will to rob. He was talking about values and ethics. After a lengthy brain washing, wooing in with a major share, they could persuade him. His demand for 50% of the share was agreed. On that appointed mid night, the two robbers were waiting, at the bottom of the tree and the gypsy climbed up. Without moving further, he came down after the very first step." Why are you not proceeding further?" On questioning him, he replied, "I want claps to be given, drums to be beaten. That is my practice and I am conditioned to that". The robbers got terribly disappointed". "What is the kind of job you have to execute and what are you asking for?". The task was given up and they were on the look out for a more suitable person ....

You may say that gypsy could not be motivated by money. He was longing for appreciation, recognition…so on and so forth. Fine, that is one way of looking at.

Yet another angle, with which we can approach the whole episode is, from the purview of a team task (setting aside the example as being negative, keeping in mind, of the lessons to be learnt). The gypsy has the requisite skill (application of knowledge) of carrying out the assigned task but not the proper will (application of mind) to execute. For the successful completion of any task, one requires the requisite skill coupled with the desired will. Lack of any one will lead to the failure, on the part of the job completion. Possession of one, without the other, won't benefit either the individual, or the team he or she belongs to.

In the episode cited, the gypsy, despite his being equipped with the requisite skill could not execute the assigned task, due to his lack of will in proceeding with the task.

There are many gypsies in many organisations – in families, factories, offices and societies-who are not willing to engage their mind for the task in question. An intelligent student who does not sit to study, a skilled employee, who by his or her own nature, or with the instigation, by the problem creators, does not meet the expectations from the boss, a nation with abundant skilled human resources, but without the proper attitude, to work – instances can be multiplied for these kind of ***'gypsies'*** Their will and skill don't go together. They are like a square plug in a round hole, the purpose is not served.

With these type of individuals, their individual aspirations take prominence, pushing the team goals to the backseat, despite their knowing fully, that their aspirations can't be fulfilled in their present teams or organisations. They long for the impossible and their competence is not capitalized, either for their good or for the benefit of their organisations.

An IT employee who longs for 9–5 job, or a worker employed in a continuous running hazardous industry, aspires for A/C room job, a fresher with MBA marketing willing to work only for customer relations job and without the basic interest of working for sales, citizens of a developing nation, without the right attitude, expecting the Government to do everything for them – are we not witnessing these kinds of people?

We cannot expect mangoes, sitting under an orange tree. Why can' t we change the attitude and put our skill and will together, to get more oranges from the same orange tree, under which we are sitting, instead of expecting the mangoes, which is next to impossible?

Like the gypsy, who was longing for recognition and appreciation which is not possible and who ultimately lost the big share, due to his inappropriate attitude, many in today's environment are aspiring for the impossible and become the losers.

A recent HR study reveals that, productivity in Indian organisations can be increased by 30 to 40% on an average, without any additional investment or employing any new technology, but by merely changing the attitude of the people. The attitude or the willingness or the will, whatever name you may assign to it, is the major impediment in many individuals that stands in the way of their personnel productivity. Their capabilities are not utilised to the fullest extent or at least to the desired level.

How many heads of the families, in spite of their capabilities, but with a negative attitude towards their organisations are not progressing in their career and not earning enough to support their families?

How many employees in a number of organisations, are not fully putting forth their personnel productivity, to achieve their organisational goals?

How many departments of lots of organizations are not able to contribute to their organisational goals, despite the skills, possessed by their employees?

How many states or countries with outstanding capabilities of their people, are not progressing well?

The answer to all the above, lies in one quality – the will of the concerned people.

Unspent money devalues, idle machinery disintegrates, unutilized time dies, so also the unused potential.

The main obstacle, that stands in the effective use of the capabilities of the people, is the will or the attitude of the people.

If the leader of any team taps the right attitude of the people working with, then the organisational effectiveness can be enhanced in larger proportions.

It is not the intelligence, but the direction of our intelligence, that determines the pace of the progress. That direction is possible, only with the right attitude. This is applicable for individuals, organisations and also for nations.

Japan is a very positive example, in that direction and our own country is obviously a negative example, though it is a bitter fact, to be digested with.

Inculcating the right attitude, in tune with the organisational goals, making the individual goal subordinate to the organisational goals, are all needed in today's environment, marked by intense and very tough competition.

Distinct Personality:-

While we have seen about the attitude in general, here is an example of an employer, who stands apart. One of the many unsung heroes, in the organizational world:-

The HR head of a top notch IT company delivered a very special convocation address in Coimbatore, at KPR Mills. It is indeed a convocation, for their women workers, under their Employee Development Programme.

Many have contributed excellent case studies on Employee Development. But, this actual practice in that mill will surpass everything. The Chairman, K. P. Ramasamy, took a silent revolution, in his organization, after his interaction with the woman employees about the welfare measures. It was inferred by him, that many joined the mill out of sheer poverty despite their intention to study further. That was indeed trigger for him to provide a free higher education

The girls, working on a 8 hour shift, if interested, can study further 4 hours every day. Class room, teaching staff, computer lab and all infrastructure facilities were provided. The following tangible results would speak of the success of the whole programme:-

24536 girls had, so far finished their 10th, 12th, UG, PG courses. They have their alumni, in almost all hospitals, where the girls are working as nurses, some are school teachers, some have joined the police force and the list goes on, Twenty of these girls are Tamil Nadu Open University Gold Medalists. They received their degrees and Gold medals from the Tamil Nadu Governor. To the very natural and pertinent question, would it not lead to more attrition, the Chairman gave a nice answer – that he did not want to waste his employees' human potential. His aim was to enable them, get a good degree, which they could not pursue, due to sheer poverty. Those girls, who left the mill, with a good job elsewhere, had referred girls, from their villages, thus enabling the cycle, to continue. He would use to ask the HR professionals for job assistance for the girls completing the UG, PG, which is truly unheard of, from any employer.

He is an exceptional employer, about whom, the world needs to know. It is about this man, HR Professionals need to learn. KPR mills has been doing a silent social revolution, about which story, message should reach many.

Mentoring - Old Wisdom for Organisational Excellence

Who is your fallback, makes all the difference. Hence, choose a right fallback

Mentors Mentioned in Scriptures:-

King Janaka was a mentor to Suga, who later became Suga Brahma Rishi. Lord Krishna was a mentor to Arjuna. If queen Kaikeyi was agreeing to the throne of Rama, we would not have got Ramayana, the great Epic. If Arjuna fought immediately at Kurushetra battle field, we would not have got Bhagavat Gita. It was taught to a Kshatria not to a vysya or Brahmin or Sutra. Why because, the duty of a Kshatria was to fight. He failed in his duty, when he put down his weapons. To hammer on his head his assigned duty, Lord Krishna taught Gita. A cow, before giving milk to mankind, first gives milk to its calf. Same way the essence of Gita was first given to Arjuna and then to all mankind Whatever teachings taught to Arjuna in Gita, are even now applicable, to the corporate owners and managers (in addition to the precious teachings on Spirituality)

The Principles are Enumerated in Brief:-

1. To get rid off the unproductive qualities like Rajas and Tamas and to inculcate the most important quality Sathvik, in thoughts, words, deeds, "I", the self centered should be got rid off, which is a tamasic quality. We – the Sathvic quality should be acquired

2. Overconscious or over concentration on results will not achieve results. Rather, concentration on the process will enable one to achieve results
3. Moksha as taught in Gita is like the superordinate or higher order goal in organizations. All employees should aim to achieve the above organizational goal not confining to their department or unit goal.
4. S(W)LOT strength, limitations (weakness), opportunities and threats. This analysis is applicable for individual employees and the organization. The whole of Gita centres around the individual limitations and its overcoming.
5. Courage to change things and accepting to the things that cannot be changed are the two important qualities that are mentioned in Gita. Accept the self defeat and unlearn rather than sticking on to it.

What is applicable to Arjuna is also to all of us, since we are in some form or way are like Arjuna in our practical life.

In that way, mentoring is required not only for Arjuna, but to all of us.

Mahaperiva Teaches us, the Mentoring Concept, in a Different Dimension:

If we drop a stone in a river, it will immerse. If the same stone is tied to a wooden log, with a rope and dropped into the same river, it will float. He compares the river, to the worldly worries, or samsara sahara. We are like stones. God comes like a wooden log to us to free us. If we are firmly tied to the wooden log through the rope of bhakthi or devotion, we are freed.

Here, employees (mentee) are compared to' we', River to problems or issues faced by us, wooden log as the mentor and rope is the mentoring process. As God Almighty is there to rescue the devotees, mentors are there to free the mentees from the problems, they face.

Mahaperiva Teaches Us also a Very Important Management Principle:

When Sivasankaran, a long-standing devotee of Sri Matam came for darshan one day, an attendant treated him very harshly. Sivasankaran was very upset. He felt that he had been insulted. He was not inclined to run to Sri Maha Periyava and complain. He had, however, an opportunity to talk to Periyava. Indirectly, but intending to unburden his heart, he said with a tact, as if he were injecting a needle into a banana fruit, "Some attendants at the Matam are pronouncedly bad. They commit wrong. They covet monetary gifts. I wonder how Periyava manages with such people around him". Periyava was full of laughter. His expression seemed to suggest, "What you say is not new to me". He then began to speak, "Consider a factory where thousands work. Is everyone skilled and straightforward? Lakhs of people are working in Government offices. Everyone does not have the same level of commitment. Many do not work properly. Or if they do, they do their work imperfectly. It is not possible to send them home.

The Government has its apex body functioning. That is important. It is enough, if this apex body is alright. That much is enough. Only that much is possible. The Sri Matam is an empire in itself. Many kinds of attendants are necessarily to be found here...... Do you know Parameshwara? "Sivasankaran knew five or six gentlemen of the name of Parameswara. He blinked, not knowing which of them Periyava was referring to." I was referring to Parameshwara, the Lord of Kailasha. He has a snake around his neck. He holds fire in his hands. A wicked demon is kept under control beneath HIS feet. His retinue consists of corpses and ghosts. He roams all over the world taking all these along with him and performs his dance. If the snake were to be let loose, it will go all over the place, enjoying great freedom, frighten and bite everyone. If fire is uncontrolled, it will destroy settlements and wilderness alike. If malevolent forces are allowed to go about freely, they will attack anyone they encounter.

As for corpses and ghosts, one need hardly say anything about what they may do. Parameswara's glory lies in keeping all these evil forces within HIS control". Periyava stopped.

Sivasankaran stood in shocked silence. He had expected that Periyava would quieten him with some placatory words. But Periyava's reply sparkled with the perception of the ways of the world and was given in such unambiguous terms. It is not Sivasankaran alone, but all of us must attain greater refinement. He not only exposes the harsh reality and the right solution to face it.

It is applicable to all practicing managers and owners of enterprises.

Who is your Fallback?

In choosing a mentor, we have to be careful, People help you, through the way, they know. To help you to come out of stress, one friend will ask you to drink and another will ask you to meditate. To overcome hurt, one friend will ask you to take revenge, and another will ask you to forgive and get ahead with your life. 'Who is your fallback' makes all the difference. Duryodhana's predicament, in his own words, was, "I know what is right, but I am not able to indulge in it. I know what is wrong but I am not able to avoid it." He needed a fallback. His fallback was his uncle Sahuni, and resultantly, Duryodhana moved from bad to worse.

Arjuna's predicament was different. He was allowing his personal emotions, to dominate his sense of duty, and hence wanted to escape from the responsibilities, he had towards upholding righteousness. He needed a fallback. His fallback was Krishna, and resultantly, Arjuna was restored to his greatness.

We are all, at some point or the other, need a fallback.

Who is your fallback, makes all the difference. Hence, choose a right fallback

Management Lessons at a Merry Tour

The rising sun as well as the setting sun are both beautiful and adorable. But, in reality, the rising sun gets more respect, is even worshipped, whereas the setting sun is not given the same importance.

Golden Principles from Old:-

We were lucky enough, to have one uncle called Achu mama, (as we all, very affectionately, call him in our Apartments) as our mentor, even though he never wished to be called by that title.

We used to go merry round once in a while. We all would enjoy the scenic beauty and also his informal mentoring, during the tour, we undertook. Food for eyes, ears and mind too.

A towering personality, who is a jack of all trades and master of all too. You name a topic and he will talk for hours, that too with amusing interest. A retired HR Professional, with a hale and healthy body, even at his early eighties. He used to organise each and every tour, employing meticulous planning, with minutest details, which every working professional, should follow scrupulously.

The lesson, learnt through that tour, would reveal many management principles, taught in a very simple way.

For the recent tour to a a hill resort, he took the owner of a small restaurant, started very recently in our area, along with their cook and an assistant, for preparing the food of our taste.

The resort management did not allow us, to cook or serve the outside food, at their premises. So he fixed a mutt nearby, for preparing the food and made arrangements to serve there itself.

After the lovely and enjoyable bath at the falls, everybody was feeling hungry. The open hall at the mutt could accommodate only 25. Achu mama decided to have ladies and children for the first batch and the rest would take in the next and final batch. He would be sharp to take appropriate decisions suited to the circumstances. When the first batch was about to complete the lunch, he was seen talking to the servant maid in the mutt, presumably to arrange for the clearing of the used banana leaves. It seemed, that she was not prepared for that, by quoting the mutt rules. Achu mama was searching for the cooking assistant, who was not traceable. The next batch could come in, only after the crucial task of clearing the leaves and cleaning. Without any hesitation, Achu mama plunged into action, by leaning down and took the first used leaf. On seeing this, the restaurant owner came nearer to him and pushed him away. "Ayya! What are you doing? Please go away! We will make things ready in five minutes." On seeing this, the cook and assistant all jumped in. The task was over within five minutes and all had a delicious food. What should have turned into an unpleasant situation in that hungry mood was very cleverly averted by his quick and timely action. A leadership lesson was taught by him in a subtle way through his action. He explained that leadership concept, when we were assembling in the evening.

Suit to the Situations:-

"I call this as situational leadership. I would have waited for the servant to come and clean the area. At that hungry moments, it was very natural that all would have cursed me. Hence I plunged into action, not with gimmicks, but with a clear intention. A leader has to lead from the front at the crucial situation. Without pushing from the back, he has to pull all by acting from the front. You might call me a leader or not, but I had a firm will to do justice for the role, I voluntarily took for the tour. He should have high integrity.

Talking about the **ownership attitude of a leader,** he was quoting an incident that happened to his friend. His friend worked as an assistant editor of a leading magazine, under the chief editor who was a giant in his field. When there was a blunder in one of the published articles, which invited contempt of court, the editor was called to appear in the court. He did appear and he did not even utter a single word to the assistant editor, who was responsible for editing that piece of article. That assistant editor accompanied him to the court on a guilty note. When he asked him "why are you keeping mum sir, please scold me a few words". the editor immediately responded "when the matter has gone to print it is my responsibility. It is my mistake that I have not corrected it, when it comes to my table. For my own mistake, why should I take you to task?." After narrating this event he went on further saying "there are people like him, who own up the responsibility. Taking the case of today's incident, I should have doubly checked up the arrangements and all the facilities and assistance available. I committed a mistake, in not foreseeing the mutt rules for employing the maid for cleaning. **For my own mistake, why should I make others hungry.?** That is why I leaned down and initiated for the clearing of leaves.

Manager or Leader:-

What is the basic difference between a manager and a leader? To this question from him, many gave different answers. But he had put it very simply as:

Manager-manage-r managing the–r–the resources, the five resources, five 'M's – Men, Machine, Money, Material and Methods or technology. He should manage all the five properly.

Leader-lead-e-r lead in effective use of resources, why effective not efficient? Effectiveness is result oriented, efficiency activity oriented. Not all activities will lead to the desired results.

In any organization, we require the combination of both – manager, who should be technically strong in his designated field, by using his given authority, which is positional, and leader who has to get the desired results, by using his power which is purely personal, which is his unique characteristic, that cannot be given by the organization. He himself has to strive to acquire it. Where to use the authority, where to use the power is the real acid test for an individual official.

There is no quick fix formula to derive the percentage of these two functions. Whether the cat is black or white, it has to catch the rat. The official has to get results without compromising the relationship.

Organisational managers get struck up with activity trap, which they relish, spending their major time, in their routine, fire fighting jobs, without spending time, for the future plans. They also fall victim to Parkinson law of triviality, where they spend more time, on trivial matters, without focus on vital and important things. They feel comfortable with routine and known things, without bothering to allot time to update themselves, with the latest developments in their field. As a result the organizations fall behind their shrewd competitors.

Another thing is – they are unwilling to take action against the problematic employees. They are like Arjuna in Mahabharatha, who was talking about Ahimsa. As a Kshatria, Arjuna should not talk about Ahimsa, when he has to fight against his enemies.

If a judge is unwilling to pass on orders to punish a criminal, he is not fit to be a judge. If a surgeon is not ready to do surgery for his patient, he is unfit to be in the medical profession. If a lady is afraid of the labour pain, she should not have become pregnant. Same way, a manager has to take disciplinary proceedings against an arrogant employee, or else he is unfit to be in the organizational hierarchy.

To put it in a simple way, ahimsa can be followed, if it is allowing a temporary pain, for permanent results.

He then cautioned the younger generation on the possible jealousy cropping up in their career. Instead of being jealous on the people, who get quick promotion, they need to find out the qualities, they possess, which are deficient in them. They should get inspired by those and try to develop those. Without proper SWOT analysis, they should not try to overtake others-be it acquiring additional qualification, changing the organization or career etc – which will have serious consequences.

Leadership Styles

After a while, he asked the following question and gave the answers in his own style:

What are the differences between Lord Rama and Lord Krishna in terms of leadership style?

With his assertive and articulated voice, even at that age, he started his lecture: "Both Rama and Krishna fought for the victory over the evil. In Ramayana Lord Rama was pulling the vaanaraas or monkeys to the land of the enemy. His loyal followers scrupulously followed him. He formed the strategy and the necessary directions as well. It was no surprise that they got succeeded in achieving the desired goal.

What about Krishna? He oversaw Pandavas, to defeat Kauravas in the battle at Kurushetra. Also Krishna told Arjuna, that he won't take part in the fight directly and employ any weapon. He would only be there as Arjuna's sarathy – on his chariot as a charioteer. He kept his words. He made Pandavas win the crucial war

What was the difference between these two leaders in their managerial style, with the type of followers being led? Lord Ram was leading an army, not so skilled fighters, , requiring proper guidance. Krishna was mentoring a highly skilled archer, Arjuna, who had confusion in his mind to fight or not against his kith and kin. While

Rama's job was that of teaching the skill, Krishna's job was that of instilling the proper will to fight and enable him to see things from an entirely different perspective Krishna worked with the highly skilled warriors like Arjuna His job was to give clarity in action without giving room for emotions and sentiments.

Coming to your family role, have you looked at your family as a team? What type of leader or parent role you are playing? Are you the one who goes on micro managing or asking the pertinent questions from your kids, so that they themselves are enabled to find their own solution? Are you playing the role of Rama or Krishna? All depends upon the intellectual and emotional maturity of your kids. Are you falling **under the category of someone, who directs all the time or under the category of someone, who clarifies doubts, allows your kids, to find their own ways.?** These are some issues and concerns pertaining to your family.

On the organisational front, are you the manager of the monkeys in your team and your ways of dealing with it? Are you the ones with the experts in their area, getting stuck up with issues? Please ponder over."

After stopping for a while, he asked one of the participants Latha to come to the front. He was asking her, to narrate one specific episode, pertaining to a servant maid, that occurred six months back, in her house.

Latha was looking for a servant maid for her house. One lady in her late forties, recommended by her friend turned up. Latha was explaining the duties and responsibilities to the old maid. Three bedrooms to be swept and mopped daily. Dishes have be washed. No dish washer, only manual. Clothings have to be washed. She was taking her near the washing machine. Until then everything was going smooth. On showing the washing machine, she said, until last month they had fully automated machine. Because of frequent failures and costly replacements, they have recently switched over to semi automated one. She was physically pointing out 'this is wash tub. this is dry tub.this is wash knob' and so on. Without allowing her to proceed further, the maid suddenly interrupted to say "Stop! I know all these! I have operated even fully automated ones. This is nothing. If you have this kind of attitude, sorry, I am not interested to work here. Please leave me" Latha was having a tough time to convince her. Of course that maid was doing a good service for a year. One fine morning she stopped coming saying that she got an assignment in a hotel. To the luck of Latha, she got an alternative – this time a young girl in her early twenties-seeming to be without much experience. The same process of briefing about the roles and responsibilities – but Latha had the conspicuous awareness of the banging from the previous maid. Without telling anything about the washing machine, she went inside after assigning the job. After half an hour, when she returned, to her shock she noticed the huge foam coming out of the gutter. With the opened water tap for the machine, with the drain knob in opened condition, all the washing liquid was coming out of the washing machine. "What did you do"? For this question from Latha the maid retorted "what should I do? I have heard about it. I don't know the operation of this washing machine. You have not told me anything."

At this stage of Latha's narration, Achu mama interrupted and invited comments from all, on the two episodes. Lot of answers came.

He summed up and said "**in both the cases she was wrong.** She **was treating the experienced servant maid with the assumption of not knowing even the basics**. By giving the unnecessary instructions, she was in fact irritating her. She should have simply delegated the responsibility which should have done the purpose. Have we not heard this oft repeated statements, in many organizations, by the older employees, controlled by younger officers" **Please stop!your age is my experience**. I know how to carry out this task. Don't irritate me, by too much of instructions." **Age and experience have to be given respect, of course without compromising the productivity**. In the second case, with the inexperienced servant maid, the house wife **took it granted on the possession of the requisite skill by the maid, without giving**

the required instructions. That resulted in the wastage of the resources. In both cases she should have assessed the skill of the servant maids, prior to the communication, regarding the job instructions. A leader therefore requires the accurate perception of the task to be completed, the person to undertake that specific task etc and then only, he has to make the required direction. **Accurate perception and correct expression are the hall marks of an effective leader.** We were all convinced by his debriefing.

Intuitive Power

He also explained simply, about **the intuitive decisions**. He narrated one incident about a recruitment process in a company, for which he was called as one of the board members. All the other five, were favouring a particular candidate for selection, with whom he was against. His intuition said that he was not fit for the post. As the chairman of the board, he vetoed them and that candidate was rejected. It was learnt that particular individual was a cheat and he had been rejected by many companies.

He termed this as intuitive decision and managers, sometimes have to go by intuition, for best results. He also cautioned against emotional decisions which should totally be avoided by managers.

Keep Right

Achu mama then poured questions to the children in the group:

Can you convert 9 into 6 by a single line? Many tried and failed. He finally came with an answer:

Nine can also be written as IX. We confine our thinking to write as only numerical nine Then if we add S before that we get SIX. When told single line, we restrict ourselves to straight line. No conditions put as single straight line. 6 can also be written as a word. All of us are acting from our left side of the brain, which is logical. But if we start using right side of our brain, then we are thinking out of the box, or lateral, or creative thinking. Putting these critical or logical thinking, along with creative thinking we can get solutions for so many problems. For that we don't require IQ. A person with low IQ can also be creative. **The pity is average human beings use only 0. 5 to 1% of our right side of the brain, while they use 10–15% of the left side. There are lot of scopes of using the right side by attempting to solve these types of puzzles.**

Activity Management

He further added, that the term **time management is a misnomer**.' How sir?' Many raised their eye brows. He said "we cannot manage time. Whether you manage it or not, it would pass as it is. But we should manage ourselves with respect to time. **So, time management is purely self management** for managing the daily activities

For that you have to follow,

5, 4. 3 formula which is THINK ,PLAN, ACT , which stand for 5, 4, 3, letter words. If we start plunging into action, without proper thinking and planning, we would only waste our time.

Next is **SIXER CONCEPT** , which is jotting down the six important things to be carried out on a particular day. Finish as per the plan. If not find out the reasons for that.

Last is **DIN attitude or DO IT NOW attitude**, without postponing. This postponing or procrastination is the thief of our time."

Change Management:-

After that, he said 'now, I am going to take you **virtually to Choluteka bridge"**. For his question, 'what is this choluteka bridge', since nobody was ready with an answer, he himself gave the details:

"Cholutica bridge was situated in a region in USA called Honduras, notorious for hurricane It was constructed in 1998, with such an engineering marvel, that it can withstand any natural calamity. The pity was, before inauguration of that bridge, a severe Hurricane called Mitch devastated the entire area. Though the bridge survived, in perfect condition, the roads on both sides completely vanished. More so, the cholutica river, totally changed its way and the bridge, constructed for it became a bridge which all called as "bridge to no where". The take away from this is, **we focus on solution for the problem. But sometime, we may forget the fact that the problem itself may totally change**. We may evolve a product or service, with utmost precision and sophistication, but **we may lose sight that the requirements might itself will change and the market itself may vanish"**

He added further "We can also give examples, from our Indian Industry, about the products like **Dyanora, Kodak Film and Ambassador car**. Those were very good products of their time. Those companies never adapted to the requirements of the customers, their tastes and preferences Whether it is an individual, or an organization, this foreseeing and adaptation to change are the imperative needs of today's cut throat competitive world. In another 10 years, many organizations like Insurance, Real Estates, Automobiles will get severely affected. No need of owning a car – with an SMS, satellite operated driverless car will come before you and take you to the destination. The role of doctors, lawyers will be reduced, replaced with Artificial Intelligence An app called tricoder can scan you and give your medical report and treatment. No need to go to a doctor. Only in – patients to go to clinics. In spite of that, we are not changing our educational system to adapt to the external environment. **What a student studies in the college is invariably irrelevant for his job. There should be total revamp of our curriculum."**

Fused Bulbs

With all these assertions and without any hesitations, he said finally ' **Iam a fused bulb '**

All reacted quickly, no! no! sir!

He said" Don't be emotional! I am only a fused bulb. Pl listen to this too!"

A senior executive retired and shifted, from his palatial official quarters to a retirement community, where he owned a house. He considered himself big and never talked to anyone. Even while walking in the community park every evening, he ignored others, looking at them, with contempt.

One day, it somehow transpired that an elderly person sitting beside him, started a conversation, and they continued to meet. Every conversation was mostly a monologue with the retired executive harping on his pet topic,

'You all don't know the very high position, I held in that MNC as its. CEO', and he started boasting about his powers. The elderly person used to listen to him quietly.

One day the, elderly listener said, "After retirement, we are all like fused bulbs, irrespective of the wattage, or glittering. After it gets fused, all these are nothing.". He continued, "I have been living in this society, for the last 10 years and have not told anyone that I was a Member of the Railway Board.

On your right, over there is, Mr. X , who retired as a top executive of Tata group. Over there is Mr. Y, who was a Major General in the Army. That person sitting on the bench, in spotless white dress is, Mr. Z who was the chief of BARC before retirement. He hasn't revealed it to anyone, not even to me, but I know."

"**All fused bulbs are now the same - whatever its wattage was - 0, 10, 40, 60, 100 watts - it doesn't matter now**. Neither does it matter, what type of bulb it was, before it got fused - **LED, CFL, Halogen, Incandescent, fluorescent, or decorative**. And that, my friend, applies to you too.

The day you understand this, you will find peace and tranquility even in this community. The rising sun as well as the setting sun are both beautiful and adorable. But, in reality, the rising sun gets more respect, is even worshipped, whereas the setting sun is not given the same importance.

It is better to understand this sooner than later. **Our current designation, title and power are not permanent.** Keeping a lot of emotions, with these things, only complicate our life when we lose this one day. **Remember, when the Chess game is over, the king and the pawn go back to the same box".**

Enjoy what you have today. Have a fabulous time ahead.

With that Achu mama concluded "Hope Iam making sense. Iam surely not that specific egoistic person."

All clapped.

If the old people understand, chew and digest these, the Bliss and Peace will be theirs. Why only old? Even youngsters, when they are in a community living, their official designations, should never come into the picture. If not, they will not only spoil their peace, but that of others.

Reflections:-

Reflections:-

Social Wellness

A selfless act will be blessed by God in multiples. In that blessing, HE will go in search of the person.

Selfless Service

Centre Stage

We have been seeing the different wheels of life – viz Physical, Mental, Family, Career, Social and Spiritual – to balance, in order to get Peace and Bliss. Among these, the Bliss and Peace, one gets in the first four are only temporary – it may vary, it may go ups and down. But, that got in Social and Spiritual will have a relatively stable outcome. It has been scientifically proved that the Happiness chemicals secreted in Social and Spiritual wellness have a long lasting effect. In that way, those assume higher significance.

It is imperative that we should do our assigned duty to the family – family first – then only to society. That however, does not mean that we should stop with our family. It should transcend beyond that. All the other wellness mentioned above have a bearing on social wellness – that a person with good physique can do service, to the needy in terms of his knowledge and skill gained in the physical part. A person with good mental wellness need to share that thoughts to the persons affected in that area. A person well versed in family wellness can share his success stories to the families affected in that arena. A person, successful in his career/business can share that secrets to the needy people who require his guidance. A spiritual person can share the spiritual wisdom to those who require for it.

Service to Athithi – Service to People in Heaven

Athithi, as they are called in Hindu Religion, mean the persons who come without any notice-(thithi means a particular timing of a day-athithi the opposite) In today's hurly-burly world, nobody entertains a person, coming without any notice. But we can plan our service, depending upon our time affordability in terms of our money, mental and spiritual knowledge. In that way, social wellness is interlinked with all the other five wellness.

All the religions preach about helping in cash or kind. Dhaanam and dharma are mentioned in Hinduism. Dhaanam is done with some expectation, in return or with some purpose, whereas dharma is done without any expectation. It is believed in Hindu Religion, the dharma we do in one birth is carried over to the successive births or to the generations of the donor.

Christianity talks about dhasama bhaagam or 10% of one's income for the needy. The holy Bible says that, ***It is in giving that we receive: as we give abundantly, we reap abundantly***. The money donated, will be given back in multiples.

Buddhism talks about tithing, given in **monetary forms.** The World Pranic Healing Foundation founded by Grand Master Choa Kok Sui stresses more on tithing, which will enhance one's spiritual development process.

What Mahabharata Says Bible also Says

There are innumerable stories, told in Mahabharatha, by many Saints to the Pandavas, while the five brothers were in exile for 12 years.

A poor little boy was with his widowed mother. Daily the son would go for begging for rice to the villagers and give whatever he got to the mother. The mother would cook all the rice and give to the needy as food and the balance would be consumed by them. The boy had a serious doubt in his mind on this practice. One day the little boy asked her mother, why she cooked all the rice, she could as well save it for the rest of the days. She replied that he was too young to understand the significance and a day will come that he would learn about the reason. The little boy not convinced went out of the house and decided not to return to his house, unless he found the answer to his doubt. It was very dark when he reached a forest. A hunter met him on the way, asked him not to venture in to the dark inside the forest, since he would be eaten by the wild animals. He asked his wife, who was at the top a tree, which was used by them as a dwelling place to stay. His wife was not relished to entertain the boy. She gave only one piece of thinai (millet) the other one she ate. The hunter gave that to the little boy and gave a little space available to the boy, leaving very very little space for himself to sleep. The next day morning, the little boy heard the loud and huge cry of the lady. Her husband, the hunter fell down from the tree and had been eaten by an wild animal. Fed up with the incident, he continued his mission to find the answer for the doubt. He met a Saint and narrated all to him. The saint told him to go to the kingdom nearby, where he would get the answer. He reached the place. He heard that the queen was about to give birth to a baby. With very much courage and wisdom on his face, he asked the people to take him to the king. The king saw his sparkling eyes. He told the king to bring the new born child in a golden plate. The king was astonished to hear and he did the same. The nurses, who attended the Queen, told the king that the child was very pretty, but it did not cry as done by any normal child. The little boy told the king, that he would ask one question to the child and then he would cry. He asked the same doubt, haunting his mind, to the child. The answer came immediately from the child, which astonished the entire courtyard:

Aththinaikku iththanaiyaanaal athhanaikkum ethanaiyaakum?

It means that a small piece of thinai given to the boy, in need (millet) has made the hunter to be born as a prince to the king, what should be for the daily dharmam, made by the poor mother of that young boy.?

The boy was glad to get the answer, for the doubt and went to his mother to tell the news. He was very happy to be united with his mother.

A selfless act will be blessed by God in multiples. In that blessing, HE will go in search of the person.

A priest in a village. informed the people, that God had prepared the list of 100 people, with whom HE was satisfied, through their service to the needy. Many were eager to see the list, to find out, if their name was finding a place. One such person, who did yeomen service to the needy, was disappointed, that his name was not there in the list. He asked the priest why? The priest replied that God had HIS own list, in which HE has chosen some, whom HE HIMSELF will come and see in person. That person was in that list. If we take up the work of God HE will come and gratify them in person. If we work with God, HE will work in our favour. It is not that HE is working for us, it is HE who works with us. That is through our acts, doing our best, for the needy

Worship the Nature:-

God created panchaboothas – Soil, water, fire, air, sky – for the well being of all human and other beings. The soil gives many vital & micro nutrients. Water is the universal solvent and is of utmost importance. The sun gives rain by evaporation of water. It gives vitamin D , poorer we are that we are not utilising that, instead spends money to get artificial Vitamin D. It is our earnest duty to keep those five intact, as created by HIM. Social wellness includes, keeping the above five intact, without polluting them. The earth we stay, is the shelter given by GOD to dwell. The rent we have to pay for that shelter, is to keep it safe, to reserve for the future generations. We should ask this pertinent question to ourselves – *Are we doing our duty to these panchaboothas as expected by GOD?*

Once a farmer and his wife approached Mahaperiava, Kanchi Mahan. They regretted that they did not have time to go to temples and pray to God, since they were to leave very early in the morning and they would return, only after sun set. The Mahan told them, not to worry, since their duty is worth to go to temples and their acts feed the mankind. It would be enough, if they prey Sun God, while starting in the morning and while returning from their work. That will suffice. Doing one's duty and worshipping one Panchaboothas would be equivalent to worship at the temples. The very feeling that they were not able to go to temples, would itself be enough. Mahaperiava pacified them.

Are you a Sea of Galilee?

As said earlier, it is in giving that we receive. A spring supplying water, to the nearby people, will be replenished with more water, for being supplied, to more needy

There is an old story, about two seas in Israel, one fresh and the other one very salty.

It is so salty that only bacteria and microbial fungi can survive in it. It has salt content, ten times more than sea water. It is said that both these seas have their source from the Jordan River. But the Sea of Galilee is vibrant and alive, while the Dead Sea, at the lowest altitude on Planet Earth has no outlet to flow. So the sea of Galilee has an outlet; it flows outward into the Jordan River while the Dead Sea can only receive and does not flow outward.

Moral from these two waters is that, those who give, prosper, while those who keep everything for themselves, dry up and whither. By giving to others, we actually keep ourselves growing to prosperity. Giving and sharing bring positive vibrations in our life. Those who keep everything with themselves are called as ***Lobi in Hindu scriptures.***

Not Pompous but Simple-

In practical life we see many people, who donate cash and kinds, purely with publicity motive. They may give X amount, for a cause. But they will spend multiples of that x, for making it publicised. To quote an example, when a person donating a few tube lights to a temple, the money, he spends for making his name visible in the tube lights and other publicity activities will be much more than the actual cost of the lights.

God does not relish these kinds of display but he likes only simplicity. A real life example that happened in 8th century A. D. will reveal that. There was an ardent devotee of Lord Shiva in a place called Thiruninravoor (near Chennai now). He saw a statue of Lord Siva in an open place. He approached a lot of people for donation to construct a temple for the Lord. But he could not get. He thought, he could construct a temple in himself. He mentally prepared a blue print and then proceeded with the mental construction, based on his blue print. After the entire construction was over, he thought of doing the Kumbhabishekam, the consecration ceremony. He prayed to God to come and adorn the statue. It so happened that a Pallava King was also fixing the consecration ceremony on the same day, for another temple, built by him. The Lord appeared in his dream and told him that HE could not come, since there would be another temple ceremony, fixed at the same time. The king got upset and went to the place. The king was given the name of the person by God. So he asked his people to search for the person. To his surprise, no function in that village was being held. He could spot a saivite called Poosalar, contemplating in his mind at his house. Upon enquiry, the king was told the story, that the person was building temple in his inner mind and for that only the function was just over. The king prostrated before Poosalar and he asked him to give the blue print, with which he could build a temple. The story went like that. The crux of the story is that God is not for luxury, but was for real devotion with modesty.

The same thing happened for the famous King Raja Raja chola of 10th century A.D, during which he built the renowned Brahadheeswara temple. The support for the kalasam, at the Gopuram for the sanctum sanctorum,' could not be properly located. It was Lord Shiva, who came in the dream of the king that it was available, with the old lady who was supplying free butter milk for the workers, involved in the construction. It was a simple pestle and mortar, used by the old lady in her kitchen. The Lord also later told in his dream, that piece gave a good shelter than the one given by the king. The king was very surprised and went to honour the old lady. This anecdote also vindicated that, God is not enamoured by luxuries and he will be pleased only with real devotion by noble minds

Honesty without Helping Tendency - 'KOMBUTHEN'

The society is the sum total of individuals. Change in an individual, will lead to the change in society.

While God is there, seeing every act of human beings, we should see that our actions are, with extension orientation. We are seeing many people, with perfect honesty. But they will be simply honest, quoting the rules and regulations, without taking efforts to help the needy. Those people are like '**KOMBUTHEN'(h**erd of honey at the topmost branch of a tree). It is of no use to anybody. These honest people without helping tendency, are like this type of honey-herd, doing nothing for the people, who come to them for help. Without merely quoting the rules and regulations, if they are bending the rules (not for any selfish motive, but for the good of the needy) without breaking the rules, their names will be remembered by many and they will be blessed by them. I have come across with such rare people in my life, who were not rigid, but flexible enough to help, at the need of the hour. I salute those people even now.

Those people are perfect examples, for fulfilling the command, from their conscience. At this juncture, ***I recall a poem by Ram Jethmalani, a renowned lawyer.***

Sometimes in the dark of the night,
I visit my conscience
To see if it is still breathing,
For its dying a slow death
Every day.
When I pay for a meal in a fancy place,
An amount which is perhaps the monthly income
Of the guard who holds the door open.
And quickly I shrug away that thought,
It dies a little.
When I buy vegetables from the vendor,
And his son "chhotu" smilingly weighs the potatoes,
Chhotu, a small child, who should be studying at school.
I look the other way
It dies a little.
When I am decked up in a designer dress,
A dress that cost a bomb
And I see a woman at the crossing,
In tatters, trying unsuccessfully to save her dignity.
And I immediately roll up my window.
It dies a little.
When I buy expensive gifts for my children,

On return, I see half clad children,
With empty stomach and hungry eyes,
Selling toys at red light
I try to save my conscience by buying some, yet
It dies a little.
When my sick maid sends her daughter to work,
Making her bunk school
I know I should tell her to go back.
But I look at the loaded sink and dirty dishes,
And I tell myself that is just for a couple of days
It dies a little.
When I hear about a rape
or a murder of a child,
I feel sad, yet a little thankful that it's not my child.
I can not look at myself in the mirror,
It dies a little.
When people fight over caste creed and religion.
I feel hurt and helpless
I tell myself that my country is going to the dogs,
I blame the corrupt politicians,
Absolving myself of all responsibilities
It dies a little.
When my city is choked.
Breathing is dangerous in the smog ridden metropolis,
I take my car to work daily,
Not taking the metro, not trying car pool.
One car won't make a difference, I think
It dies a little.
So when in the dark of the night,

I visit my conscience
And find it still breathing
I am surprised.
For, with my own hands
Daily, bit by bit, I kill it, I bury it.

This is the honest confession, by a renowned person. We ourselves have to introspect in loneliness, try to correct us, for our little contribution to the society. The society is the sum total of individuals. Change in an individual will lead to the change in society.

Five is Greater than Six

The picture needs no explanation. Animals with only five senses, are better than the men with so said 'sixth sense'

How many of us are following the lane discipline on the public path?

How many of us have the road sense?,

How many of us take care about the wastage of food – be at home or at restaurants?

In this world of making money and earning fame, we are driving away the humane attitude.

Who is Mentally Retarded?

A dozen small girls were standing on a track for racing. With the signal,, all girls started running.

Hardly had they covered only a small distance, one girl slipped and fell.' Because of pain, she started to weepWhen other11 girls heard her cry, all of them stopped for a few seconds. To the surprise of everybody, they turned back towards the girl, lifted her, gave their consolation, all walked together and landed on the winning post. This incident moved all. This incident happened at Pune conducted by National Institute of Mental Health, as the race for the mentally retarded.

The basic truth from these so called mentally retarded are:

- ***Team working***
- ***Care and concern***
- ***Compassion***
- ***Sympathy***
- ***Selflessness***

What was done by them cannot be done by us because of our

- ***Ego***
- ***Selfishness***
- ***Complex Attitude***
- ***Uncared for the virtues by the retarded***

We still call them as retarded...

We need Good Samaritans

Among many unscrupulous people in the world, there are good Samaritans too, who strive to save the mankind. Because of those only, still we get rain.

The following are the kinds people, who are urgently needed for the course correction in the society.

An Electrician to restore the current between people, who do not speak to each other anymore.

An Optician to change the outlook of people.

An Artist to draw a smile on everyone's face.

A Construction worker to build a bridge between neighbours.

A Gardener to cultivate Good Thoughts.

A Plumber to clear the choked and blocked mindsets.

A Scientist to rediscover compassion.

A Language teacher for better communication with each other.

Last but not the least A Mathematics teacher for all of us to relearn how to count on each other.

Ultimately, the following is the need of the hour:-

The planet does not need more successful people. It desperately needs more peacemakers, healers, restorers, lovers of all kinds

Mother of 20 Children-

Here is an example of a good samritan, a dedicated nurse, Anjali Kulthe who stood, with astute commitment and dedication in saving the lives of many, on that fateful day, 26/11

On that fateful night of 26/11/2008 'Ajmal Kasab' , the treacherous terrorist, entered the premises of 'Cama Hospital' along with anther co conspirator and started firing erratically, resulting in the death of two security guards and injuring a nurse. Both were advancing further, who were watched by Anjali Kulthe, 50 year old nurse, in her 'night shift' duty. She was in charge of the maternity ward, with 20 pregnant women. When she was watching them, proceeding towards that ward, she immediately closed the very hard doors. She was so courageous to shift all the 20 pregnant women to a small pantry, with sheer dedication. How delicate and risky it was, to shift twenty pregnant women, in such an emergency? Kasab and his accomplice went to the terrace and started firing the police personnel. Anjali shifted the injured nurse to the casualty and gave the necessary first aid. At that time, one of the pregnant women, showed the signs of labour pain. Anjali made her move, with her hand and made a smooth delivery, with the help of a doctor.

She used to get scared often, after this terrible incident. When she was called, as a witness by the police, for establishing the identity of the murderer Kasab, she volunteered to come in her uniform. Reason – she realized the importance of the uniform, for a nurse, which alone could dare to take that brave act.

She not only saved the lives of 20 pregnant women, but also 20 children, who were about to enter the jaws of their fate.

Those twenty children would be 14 years old, now. They may not even aware that they have two mothers-one their physiological mother, who carried them in their womb, and the other, their guardian mother Anjali Kulthe, who actually gave life for them, just before their birth.

Let us salute Anjalitai, for her incomparable courage and resourcefulness!

We need these kinds of selfless patriots, in the society!

Family First

Charity begins at home-like wise, service should also begin at home. Without caring the family, if one does social service, it will be of no use. A lady doing spiritual practices, without caring for her ailing husband will never attain illumination. A father who teaches free for many poor students without bothering about his own son, who is poor in studies will not do any justice.

It is very clearly mentioned in Vedas that reciting Vedas by a true Brahmin, without reciting the basic Gayathri Manthra will pour only cold water.

There is a story in the Mahabharatha told by a Saint to the Pancha Pandavaas, while they were in twelve years' exile. A Brahmin by name Kausika, against the wishes of his ailing old parents went to the forest, to do penance for getting illumination. After a specific period, he assumed that he got it. At that time, an egglet dropped its excretion on his head. When he stared at the bird, it got charred. He concluded that he had got the spiritual power. With that ego, he went to the nearby village to beg for rice, as per the practice called Bhikshai, followed by a brahmachari. One lady took more time to come and offer the rice. He stared at her. She uttered immediately ***Kokkenru ninaithaayo konganavaa?*** Meaning Iam not an egglet to get charred. Shocked by her remarks, he asked her how she knew that recent incident. She said it was because of her ***Pathi Viratha Dharmam***- meaning, her service to her husband. She also advised him to go to Kaasi, the sacred place and get the spiritual advice from a person called, Dharma Vyathan. When he met him, he was annoyed to find that he was a butcher. How come a Brahmin, to get spiritual advice form a butcher? Unwillingly he asked him. That person said he did not know anything, excepting serving his ailing parents. He took him and introduced to his parents. It was at that time, it struck to the Brahmin, that he had failed in his duty as a son to his aged ailing parents. His conscience pricked him and he went back to help his parents. Better than the penance, service to the parents is of more importance and significance, he learnt that precious lesson from a butcher.

Service to Humanity is the Best Work of Life

The service to the needy with a helping hand, is better than worshipping the God with folded hands

Service Pays

Three incidents, that happened to three different families, are worth to be mentioned under this context.

Number one:

A man of 40s had his bed-ridden mother in an ICU. The doctors attending to her washed off their hands and he went to bring his wife and his daughter. On the way, he saw a young lady, with her little child, begging for food. He got some eatables, from the nearby shop and gave them to eat. The young mother raised her folded hands and blessed him. With a fulfilled mind, when he returned to the hospital, he was told by the attending nurse that miracle had happened and his mother got up in her bed. Surprised and joy-stricken, he took his mother's hand in his lap. The mother said that a young mother with her child raised her folded hands and blessed her. Tears rolled down from his eyes.

God has acknowledged his service to the needy by bringing his mother back from the jaws of death.

Number two:

A boy studying in a school, was selling clothing in the nearby places. One afternoon, he felt very hungry as well as thirsty and knocked at the door of a house, wherein a young girl was staying. He asked for water, even though he was longing for some food. That girl, upon seeing his face, brought a glass full of milk and offered him to drink. He went with much satisfaction. She gave the needed, even without being asked by him.

Years rolled down. A lady was admitted in a famous hospital for some unidentified illness. The chief of the hospital could diagnose the exact ailment and put all his efforts to save her. On treating her, he could recognise that lady, even though that lady could not recognise him. The day of discharge came. The lady with her family was keeping their fingers crossed about the hospital bill. The chief of the hospital had very clearly instructed his accounts people to send the bill before giving it to the lady. The lady got the bill with a note from the chief:

Paid in full with a glass of milk. *The lady got her eyes filled with tears.*

There is a saying: ***Send your bread out in the water, because in course of time, you may find it again***. *What goes around will come again. An act of goodness, we do today will come back to us or to those we love, at a moment, completely unexpected*

Number three:

A man in late 70s, was in complete coma for more than 5 years. Everything was done artificially. Doctors were not sure of his bodily conditions. He might survive longer or die sooner, was their answer. His son consulted a spiritual person, who said there was only one way, by which his soul would leave the body. There was no chance of his survival. He also suggested to give tithing as they call in Buddhism, the amount will be revealed by him. He closed his eyes. Asked the son of the man in coma, to imagine a sum of money starting with 1000. He started. The spiritual person in his closed eyes told "not enough". He raised to 10000. The process continued until the son said 10 lacs. That amount was asked to be donated to the most serious patient say in cancer or other diseases. He did donate. On the next day of the donation, his ailing father left the world.

The explanation given by the spiritual person was the ailing father had owed a karmic debt to somebody, unless it is repaid, the soul will not leave the body. If he had not donated that amount, till that amount is spent for the treatment expenses, he would have been in Coma. Tithing to the needy is the best form of service. Educating the needy poor, feeding the poor, helping for medical expenses of the poor person, are all satisfying God, since we are taking up HIS work.

The service to the needy with a helping hand, is better than worshipping the God with folded hands

It is in Giving that We Receive

A very rich lady with all the luxuries in her life, went to consult a counsellor.

"My life is empty, I have everything but feel I have nothing. Without any aim in my life, I don't have peace and happiness. Please show the way for me" Without giving the direct answer to her, he asked her servant maid, to come and talk to her. It was as if she was her counsellor.

She started telling her story" A few years back, I lost my husband, within 3 months. my only son too passed away. I felt the total emptiness. Six months passed by. One night, it was raining heavily. I noticed a dog at our house entrance, shivering. I took it inside and gave biscuits. After eating, it licked my leg. I felt something different. I did get enormous peace on that day.

I had noticed several times in the past, an ailing old lady in our street. I would pass by, without caring her. After the day, I cared for this dog, I started giving the share of my food to the old lady. She started blessing me. That blessings gave me more peace and happiness. I started doing that kind of little things to the needy. Now I feel, I will be the most happiest person in this world. Happiness springs when you help the needy."

The counsellor told the lady "hope you got the real counselling from her. Happiness is not something, in your being happy. But it lies in making others happy"

From the Bottom Most Heart of a Billionaire

Femi Otedola is one among the 1000 rich persons. Once, he was interviewed, with the start of the question,"Which life incident changed you, the happiest person?"

The answer given by him went like these:-

I had crossed the four stages of my life. In the first stage, my life was spent, on amassing wealth. I did not get any peace in that stage. During the second stage, I spent, for collecting the costliest things for my house. I could realize that the pleasures, I derived were only temporary. In the third stage, I expanded my shipping business, when I became the biggest ship owner in Asia and Africa. But alas, I could not get the imagined happiness, during that stage too.

In the fourth stage, I was asked by my friend, to donate the wheel chair for the handicapped children, run by an NGO. First,

Initially, I gave only money. But on my friend's compulsion, I went there, donated the wheel chairs to all the 200 children with my own hands. I could see the flashing happiness in those faces, which I could not express, but can only be experienced.

When we started leaving the place, one small child suddenly came, touched my legs with its two hands and started gripping firmly.

I asked the child" Do you want anything?"

The answer given by that child, totally changed my outlook towards my life:

"I wish to remember your face. Why because, when I am meeting you in heaven, I will take you to God, request and plead HIM to bless you with everything"

Without waiting for my reactions, she left with her friends immediately.

That was the day, I felt the divine blessings and felt more happier

Who else can be a blessed one, better than this person? What else can be a blissful moment for one, other than this?

Man is a social animal. No man is an island. The more we do for others, it will be returned by God to us, some where in our life time, because we are taking up HIS work.

This is the crux of the significance of Social Wellness.

Reflections:-

Reflections:-

Spiritual Wellness

This is the last, but not the least wheel, to be balanced by any individual.

Differences Between Religion and Spirituality-

Selfless will remember WIIIFW, meaning, what is in it for world. God will go in search of them

Many do confuse the religion with spirituality. Let us find out the basic differences between religion and spirituality:

Through religion, we differentiate ourselves as Hindus, Muslims, Christians, Buddhists Sikhs etc. But a spiritual person does not identify himself with any religion, instead unifies all, by the dictum that we are all not the body, the mind but the soul. We are all the children of Supreme God. The Supreme God has come down in different Avadhars. Each Avadhar was taken to propagate a particular philosophy and tenet. Unfortunately, only that particular tenet has been taken as everything and its followers started calling that as their religion. God created the country but we, men, have only created the towns and villages and are fighting with each other. It is disheartening to note that the children of the Supreme God are crossing swords against each other. ***The need of the hour is therefore religious harmony.***

We are not the body. We are not the mind. We are not the source. We are the soul. When a carpenter is making a furniture, the latter cannot be called as the carpenter. A computer programmer will design a programme. We cannot term all these programmes, as the computer. A body is the vehicle of the soul. It will be programmed to act according to the will of soul, which has been already programmed by the predetermined acts of fate. The thoughts, feelings, emotions are all the products of the soul which have been pre programmed already. In the Pranic Healing, Grand Master Choa Kok Sui has asked to address everybody with the saying "Atma Namaste!" treating all the others, as the souls.

Came from God and to go to God

There is a saying in spiritual circle, ***Egan Aneganaakiraan. Jeevan Sivanaakiraan.*** That sums up the entire purpose of human beings. Egan means, the Supreme God. It takes different forms, through Mayaa, illusion. As a drop of sea water tastes like the whole sea, we all, the Pinda, the micro, are like the Anda, the macro. That is the starting point of birth for all. Each undergoes different transformations, both positive and negative. Then these different forms have to come back to the Siva (Supreme God), with the original purer form, as they came initially, from the Supreme God. It takes different births – for some thousands, for some hundreds, some take a few births only, depending upon the development of each soul.

Even though we are all children of God and all are our brothers and sisters, we don't move with all amicably. Once, the renowned Saint Ramana Maharishi was asked by a devotee,"why others are not treating him properly?". He replied immediately **"who are those others?"**. All are one with God, all are products of God. Move with that thoughts. We have to evolve with that in mind The negative thoughts, emotions-all these vaasanaas, accumulated over our previous births, have to be eradicated from our mind.

If we firmly believe that, we all are children of God, then God will come in search of us.

A very impressive story on that............

Where is God?

A person was planning to go to the top of a hill temple to worship God. His mother advised him not to go with empty hand, to worship. So he went with a pocket of rice flakes, as done by the close friend of Lord Krishna, Sudhama.

When he reached the base of the mountain, he found out that there were multiple paths to reach the top. Easy way, difficult way, free way, way with fare, way with recommendation letter to go quickly. so on and so forth. There were guides in each path. Some were discouraging him, not to venture, since it would be difficult to reach the top. One told him, to give the money for Hundi and it would be deposited on his behalf. One ridiculed him that he was foolish to believe that God exists. He was confused, as to, if he had to proceed or not.

At that time, one hand stretched before him and that eyes begged for food. Without any further thought, he gave the bag with rice flakes meant for God to the beggar. He thanked him profusely. From that mouth, came the voice of God.

" What are you doing here my dear God?" That person asked.

"I am here only" came the answer.

"But then who is there at the top?"the person quipped

"Yes. I am there at the top too. Those who are not able to see me here, come to the top" response came from God

"That means you don't have any proper form"

"I don't have any fixed form. In whichever form, you wish to see me, I will come to you in that form."

"I don't understand"

"You saw me in the eyes of that beggar and also in the food you gave to that beggar. I am the giver and I am the recipient. For getting my dharshan, you don't need eyes, but a mind only"

"That means I need not come to the top to see you"

"You are free to come. Those who are not able to see me here at the bottom, as you did just now, are only coming to the top to see me"

"I don't understand"

"Understanding is not difficult. If you are living for you, you can come to the top, if you live for others, you can see me at the place you are. You need not come in search of me. I will come in search of you." God gave a big smile and stopped HIS voice.

Selfish people will remember only **WIIIFM**, *meaning* **what is in it for me** *and God will never come nearer to him.*

Selfless will remember **WIIIFW**, *meaning* **what is in it for world**. *God will go to them. Should we be interested in what? Obviously* **WIIIFW.** Naturally our actions should speak for that path.

God is Omni present. Our selfless actions will bring HIM towards us. That is the true spirit of Spirituality.

If we are feeding the poor, we are taking up the work of God. In that case We will become God in the eyes of the poor.

We have seen already that we have to come back to God, in the same form as we left HIM. The following anecdote will explain that in detail:-

It is said, that that the Soul of a person, after leaving the physical body, will argue with God, that it is not interested to take another birth in this world. God will console the soul that he will be given two chances before the birth.

One is, he can live, as his atma wishes and reach HIM finally. Second is, he can live as per his mind and be born again and again. Both choices are with him. No interference from HIM, unless he calls HIM. Every soul will remember these words of God till the seventh month of its being, in the mother's womb and will call God every now and then." Please don't make me, be born again. It will plead."

After the seventh month, Shadam, a kind of fluid, will make a layer around the fetus and make the atma forget all those, told earlier.

We can recall the Satari, that is being placed on our head, in all Vaishnavite temples. The significance of it is, to pray God, that the bad effects of Shadam should be removed and the prayer should be answered, when in womb, against the act of Shadam

We may argue that God is very cruel and HE creates obstacles to rule us. But, we conveniently forget that HE gave two opportunities, one is through atma and the other through mind. Atma is the bridge between us and the God. Mind is the bridge between us and the earth. The choice is ours.

It is mentioned in Hindu scriptures, that God lives at the right side of our heart, in 1/100 part of a grain and HE speaks as our inner voice, whenever we go wrong. If we pay heed to that, we will be safe. But many don't. HE lives in us with all our births, with the hope that we will change in any of the births. HE gives every chance to change and take us with HIM, , but the pity is that, we are not utilizing it. Same thing was explained in an anecdote, in Mahabaratha. Saint Uthava charged Lord Krishna that HE was very cruel with Pandavas. If HE had so thought, HE would have saved Yuthishtra from being deceived by Kauravas in the gambling. Lord told that it was up to Yuthishtra, to call HIM, whenever he was in trouble. HE was waiting for his call on that day of gambling. But he prayed that HE should not come. What else can HE do?

The bottom line is – it is we, who should use our atma and the inner voice, to evolve in our births, cutting the further chains.

Free Will & Karma

We should understand that one act of injustice can destroy all the good virtues, practiced over one's life time.

In that direction, we should remember, that Human Birth is the ultimate of all births and God has given us the sixth sense, to differentiate between good and bad. It is called the divine voice, which has been given a new name, as Free Will by modern management. (We have seen about Free will in the previous episodes, through a different dimension.)

One should follow Dharma, the righteousness, in one's own life. What will happen to him? Many have written the Bhashyam or the meaning of the entire Valmeegi Ramayana, the original Ramayana. One such, gives the gist of the entire Ramayana. One who follows Dharma, will be helped by even monkeys that happened to Lord Rama, who got the help of Anjeneya and all the Monkeys or Vaanaraas, as they are called. For the one, who goes against Dharma will be even ditched by his own brother, that happened to Ravana, whose brother, Vibheeshana turned against him.

Karma plays an important part in one's own life. However great one may be, for that matter even Gods have to undergo the effects of Karma.

Different Types of Karma

Even though, we have dealt with the different types of Karma in mental wellness, it is worth to repeat them, here again. One comes across three types of Karma, as described in scriptures-Sanjitha karma, Prarabhdha Karma and Agamya Karma.

Sanjitha Karma, is the sum total or accumulated karma in one's soul journey. That can be compared to all the diseases, one undergoes in one's own life. They can be compared to the total arrears, a student has to clear in his degree course.

Prarabhdha karma is the disease, that person suffers at the given situation. It can be the arrears, a student has to complete in a particular semester.

Agamya Karma, is the act one undertakes in his present situation. It can be compared to the treatment, one has to follow in combating the disease. It can be compared to the efforts, a student takes to clear the arrears.

If proper measures are taken, then the disease will go off. If sincere efforts are taken, the student will clear the arrears.

Sanjitha karma or the total disease will not be under the control of a person, so also the Prarabhdha Karma, the disease, suffered at the present moment. But the efforts taken to ward off the disease are purely under the control of one self. This Agamya Karma is similar to the Free will, coined by modern management. It is totally under the control of a person. If one utilizes the free will at the right time, his soul can evolve properly. We cannot do anything with the past deeds. But we can definitely do good deeds from the present moment and erase the negative karma gradually. As we increase the credit in our bank account, debit is decreased. Same way, as we increase the good deeds, we can minimize the accumulated bad karma.

We come into contact with many in our day to day life. Our kith and kin, relatives, friends and colleagues – each one is coming, to settle the karmic accounts-either getting lessons from us or teaching us some lessons. It would be surprising to know, if I say, a loving couple in this life, might have been like a cat and rat in one of their previous births. They are settling or nullifying the bad karma in this birth. Otherwise, the karmic accounts will not get balanced. A person with extreme lust and without satiating that, will be born as a prostitute in the next birth. A wife, who tortures her husband, will be born as a husband, to get the same torture from the other. A person, who tortures her daughter in law will be born as a daughter in law in another birth, to get the same treatment. Newton's third law of motion, will be applicable in the Karmic account too. What goes around will alone come back. God is highly impartial. At the same time, HE gives ample chances, by way of new births to each to correct so that the soul will evolve.

Mahaperiva, the Great Saint used to tell a story of a couple, who came to him for getting blessings, to get a child, since they did not have any issue, even after 10 years of married life. Mahaperiva told the lady immediately" sorry, it is not possible for you to get a child. You ill treated all your three children, blessed in the previous birth. Repent from the bottom most heart and God may bless in one of the subsequent births".

What is more important, is the honest repentance, from within and asking for pardon.

We cannot change the situations happening to us. That is like fate. But the reaction to the situation, purely lies in us. That is our choice. Through that choice, we can save us from future happenings. For example, we are walking through an unfamiliar road. There are potholes in the road. We tend to fall. That is the situation. We learn from that. We will make the choice of being more careful in future, while passing through that kinds of roads. We can avert the future happenings. This makes us to form a hypothesis as given below:-.

Accept what has happened. Don't resist. What lessons have you learnt? What will be your future course of action?

If we fully comprehend and assimilate this, then we won't have any regrets for whatever has happened to us.

A single act of injustice will spoil the entire set of previous good deeds done by one. The following anecdote from the epic Mahabaratha will explain this:

When Lord Krishna returned home, after the battle of Mahabharata, his wife Rukmani confronted him "How could you be a part of that group who killed Guru Dhrona and Bheeshma, who were such righteous people and had the lifetime of virtues behind them?"

Initially Lord Krishna avoided her questions, but when she did not relent, he replied "No doubt they had a lifetime of good qualities behind them, but they both had committed one single sin, that destroyed all their virtues"

Rukmani asked "And what was that sin?"

Lord Krishna replied "They were both present in the court when that lady (Panchali) was being disrobed. Being elders, they had the authority to stop it, but they did not. This single crime is enough to destroy all the righteousness of this world"

Rukmani asked "But, what about Karna?. He was known for his charity. No one went empty handed from his doorstep. Why was he killed?"

Lord Krishna said "No doubt, Karna was well known for his charity. He never said 'No' to anyone, who came to him. But, when Abhimanyu fell, after successfully fighting an army of the greatest warriors and when he laid dyeing, he asked for water from Karna who stood nearby. There was a puddle of clean water, where Karna stood, but not wanting to annoy his friend Duryodhana, Karna did not give water to that begging man. In doing so, the whole charity of his lifetime was destroyed. Later in battle, it was the same puddle of water, in which the wheel of his chariot got stuck and he was killed."

Rukmani could not speak further.

We should understand that one act of injustice, can destroy all the good virtues, practiced over one's life time.

Even Gods cannot escape the effects of Karma. Why? Here is the story, that was in continuation between *Threthayuga* and Dwabara yuga

After Shri Krishna killed Kamsa, he went to the jail to release Vasudev and Devki, his father and mother. Devaki asked eagerly,

"Child, you are God yourself and you have divine powers: then, why did you wait fourteen years to kill Kamsa and release us"?

Shri Krishna replied, "Respected mother, forgive me. But, why did you send me to the jungle for fourteen years in my last birth?"

Devaki was very surprised and said, "Krishna, how is this possible? Why are you saying this?"

Shri Krishna replied, "Mother, you will not remember anything about your previous birth. But you were Kaikayi in your last birth and your husband was Dhasrath".

Devki was very surprised and asked curiously, "Then, who is Kausalya now?"

Shri Krishna replied, "Mother Yashoda. The fourteen years of mother's love, that she was deprived of, in her last life, she got it in this life"

Everyone has to bear the fruits of their karma, even the Gods cannot escape from it. Keep an eye on what karma, you want to accumulate.

Peace Decoded

The mark of a true human being is not in his knowledge, but with his humility. Your intellect and education are of no use, if they feed only to your ego

Where is Peace?

Once a devotee prayed to Shri. Sathya Sai Baba "I want Peace" Baba immediately questioned "What are the three words in your sentence?" "Three" came the answer.

"Remove the first two words "I and Want". What is the remaining?" asked Swamiji.

"Peace"

That is all "Remove 'I ' , the ego and' want' , the desires from your life. You will automatically get peace.

The two things that stand in the way of attaining peace are ego and desires. If we remove those consciously from our minds, peace is rest assured.

First is Ego

After Pandavas won the Kurushetra War, Lord Krishna asked Arjuna to get down from the chariot. Arjuna, with high ego told Krishna that he was the King. Krishna as the Sarathi (charioteer) had to climb down first and then he had to escort him to the ground. Krishna got wild and shouted Arjuna to get down. As

Arjuna got down, immediately Krishna did. Soon, the whole chariot got burnt. Terrified Arjuna asked Krishna" why this?" Krishna replied "That was the reason, why I asked you to get down first. If I had, you would have been charred. As soon as I got down, Lord Anjeneya, who was protecting the chariot, with his presence as the flag, was protecting you. Without knowing those, you were commanding respect from me. Such was your ego". Arjuna stood speechless.

A similar incident happened in the life of the Great Sanskrit Poet Kalidasa

After a hectic travel, the poet reached a village. Feeling very thirsty, he was longing for water. An old lady with a bucket in her hand was spotted by him near a well.

Upon his request, she agreed to supply water, with only one condition. He should be introduced first, by giving the answer to the question," Who are you?" The egoistic poet thought, that old lady was not fit to know that he was the renowned poet, Kalidasa.

The answer came "I am a traveler"

The lady at once told that he could not be a traveler. The reason was, only the Sun and the Moon could be the traveler. Both travel permanently by rising and setting daily. She repeated the same question," Who are you?"

Perplexed poet answered "Oh! I am a guest to you"

Immediately reply came, "My dear son! There are only two guests possible in this world – Youth and wealth: Both are not permanent, even if one requests them to stay with, they won't.

'Who are you? "she was harping on the same question.

Hungry for water, but angrily the poet answered" I am a patient person."

Quick answer emanated from the old lady, "you don't seem to be a patient person. Only two are very patient in this world – earth and a tree. Whatever worst harm, you do to the earth, or hurling stones to a tree, they both feed us:" Tell me, my dear young man,, who are you?"

Irritated poet said, "I am a stubborn person"

The lady smiled and said" You don't look like that much stubborn, because there are only two such in the world – nails and hair of people. How much, we go on cutting them, they never stop growing. Tell me, Who are you?"

The Poet, who was keeping cool, so far, said with irritation, "I am a foolish person"

With a smile on her face, the old lady replied" you cannot be called as a fool. Only an incapable king and his sycophant, flattery minister are worth to be called as fools. Tell me, my child, who are you?"

The Poet Kalidasa, was now able to come down and admit, that he was overtaken by an illiterate old village woman. He surrendered to her with the most humbleness and fell at her feet. He said," forgive me, my dear Mother! I admit my ignorance. I boasted myself that I know everything. You taught me a lesson." To his surprise, he could see, there Goddess Saraswathi, who represents Learning and Wisdom and who says with utmost humbleness that still SHE is learning.

SHE said, "son! No doubt, you are wise. Wisdom without humility will lose its significance. Unless you know yourself well, you cannot become a human being. Your ego will pull down your achievements. To thwart your ego, I came. Be a true Manushya from today onwards"

The mark of a true human being, is not in his knowledge, but with his humility. Your intellect and education are of no use, if they feed only to your ego

A good Zen Story that teaches us the humility in a different perspective.

A person was approaching a Saint to learn from him. The Saint was staying at the top of a mountain. He told the person to wait for some time, since he had lots of pending jobs. The gist of their conversation is given below:-

I don't see any work to be finished. How come you say,'more work?'

I have to train two hawks and two eagles, assure two rabbits, discipline one snake, motivate a donkey and tame a lion...

Iam not able to see any of them here!

No! all are within!

The hawks look at all around me, I have to tame them, to see only the good. They are my two eyes.

The two eagles in me do harm to many and do considerable hardship. I have to educate them to be beneficial to others. Those two are my two hands.

Rabbits long to go, wherever they want, but they get fumbled, when faced with tough situations. I have to teach them to be cool. They are my feet

The donkey is not willing to carry the burden and always pretends to be tired and obstinate. I have to correct it. My body is the donkey.

The worst to control is the "snake.". Even though it is held, within the firm cage of 32 bars, it tries to injure, harm and sting those, surrounding it. I have to exercise a strong control over that. That is my tongue.

I also have a lion within. It thinks ' I am the king!' I have to put it down.! That is my ego

As you have inferred from my confession, that I have plenty of pending jobs.

The mark of a true human being is not in his knowledge, but with his humility. Your intellect and education are of no use, if they feed only to your ego

A True Lesson to be Learnt by all

As human beings, we should understand that, we alone cannot achieve anything. Manusha prayathnam (human efforts) combined with Deiva Sangalpam (grace of God) alone will bring the victory.

Same mighty Arjuna could not defeat a small army of enemies after the Kurushetra War, since Lord Krishna was not with him. The same thing happened for Bhima after the war. The same Bhima who was able to uproot the bigger trees could not move the tail of a monkey, in whom Lord Anjaneya was in disguise.

Many of us boast that saying 'I earned, I saved, I built the house, I helped, without me, he will be nowhere ' To those people, Mahaperiva, the renowned Saint posed a simple question,

Can you boast that you only make your heart function? Do you direct your kidneys to separate the toxins from your blood? Are you only digesting the food and assimilate the nutrients with the blood? Can you say that I only make the flowers blossom? Are you only responsible to ripe the fruit? Do you only make the fish, fall into the bait, while going for fishing in the sea?

Whoever does all such things is only having the eligibility and authority to utter the word' I '

So. Stop boasting the word 'I'. But, be humble without endlessly carrying your ego. Clear your

Soul surrounded and polluted by unwanted evils.

Simple Truth about Our Life

Birth, Name, Education, Income, Respect – all are given by others First and Last Bath will be given by others. After our death, our property and belongings will be taken by others. Why then Ego?Let us live with love and move with others peacefully. The journey of our life is very short. Why this ego should spoil the relationship with the significant others?

After the First, Ego Second comes Desires

Our desires are like that of the person, in the above picture. Amidst all the perils, surrounding him, he is longing for the honey, dripping from above. His mind is not towards the God, who is lending his helping hand. This is the actual state of average human beings.

Desires are plenty for the human beings, that can never be satiated. These desires lead to attachments to many things- may be animate or inanimate. Due to attachments, we develop expectations, that expectations if not fulfilled will lead to disappointment and then self pity. ***A new acronym coined by this author on this, is – AEDS***

A – attachment

E – expectations

D – disappointment

S – self pity

AIDS is a physiological disease that will kill a person gradually. This AEDS is psychological, that will also ruin a person gradually, both mentally and physically.

This attachment will be on animate as well as inanimate things:-

Towards body – We should understand that, as we grow older, we will develop problems in different parts of the body. A person at 40s cannot expect the same conditions as that of 20s and with 60 s as that of 40s. There will be degeneration of the body cells. We should accept that. We should give our best care to the body, as well as make ourselves contented, with the prevailing conditions.

Old people should reconcile that, every year above 60 years, is a bonus and we should thank God every year. Every month above 70 years, is a bonus and should thank God, every month after 70. Every day above 80 years is a bonus and should thank God, every day. The birth and death are not in our control. We should be mentally prepared for it.

With spouse – During train journey, all the co passengers will not and cannot get down at the same station. In the same way, during life journey, the co passengers – husband and wife cannot get off from the world, at the same time. If they do, they will be the most luckiest couple. One will leave earlier and the other should not make his/her life miserable, by crying over the other. There will be the misery of separation, but it should not last long. That will make their sons or daughters or other relatives in trouble. The other should devote his/her time in spirituality or service oriented activities, make the rest of the life peaceful, if not happier.

With children – It is of paramount importance, that the old parents, should stop worrying their wards' families. They should develop the thoughts, that their wards are aged and they will take care of their families. Over all guidance should only be given.

Micro management and spoon feeding should never be resorted to. Over all guidance should alone be given. There should not be any comparison with their past life, with that of the children. That will lead to misunderstanding and ultimately spoiling of relationship.

With Position and Possession – We should only love the job and not be attached to the job or the company or the boss. Otherwise we feel sad, if we are to go out of the company and the boss Some employees are emotionally attached, to the above and are landing in trouble.

Some are emotionally attached to a particular position, they are longing to get, with all their efforts. When it is not possible to fulfil that, they feel depressed. Positions and possessions are like guests, they may come to one, at any time, without notice and may leave, without bidding farewell.

Some are emotionally attached to the housing property or the vehicle they possess. When something goes wrong to those, their miseries are many

While these are the examples in the present Kali yuga, we can quote many examples in Dhwabhara yuga, with the characters in Mahabharatha.

Shanthanu's attachment to the fisherwoman called Sathyavathy, was the root cause of so many issues that cropped in in his kingdom, even after his death.

Sathyaviratha's attachment towards the kingdom of Hasthinapura, made Bhishma do many things, which were not righteous, to the man of that stature.

Acharya Dhrona's attachment towards his son Aswathama was the reason of being killed in the battle, by his own student Arjuna.

Dridirahtra's attachment towards his son Duryodhana made him carry out many unlawful and unethical acts

Sahuni's attachment towards his parents, made him perform many tasks, which were highly unethical

Pandu's attachment and lust towards his wife Mathri was the cause of so many untoward happenings in the kingdom.

So attachment towards inanimate and animate things is bound to bring forth untold miseries

Once Swami Chinmayananda was proceeding to catch a train, at a place. After reaching the station, it was known, that the train would be 30 minutes late. The persons who accompanied Swamiji, asked him to explain Bhagavat Gita. Swamiji said immediately' why 30 minutes needed? 3 seconds are enough for narrating Gita'. He said in Tamil, the whole gist of Gita as '**Edu Pidi'** which mean, remove the attachments and surrender to God. Such a very precise and nice explanation of Gita, astonished everybody.

Attachment is the root cause of all evils. That will make the common man's life very miserable Knowing fully that death is inevitable and one cannot escape, a lady was sitting before the dead body of her husband, who died at his 48 years, on the previous night. Her two children, a boy at 18 years and a girl at 15 years were sitting by her side, lamenting over the death. A highly spiritual person, close to the deceased person, came to pay homage to the body. The lady pleaded to him to bring her husband back to life, with the spiritual power, possessed by him. He was initially trying to explain the impermanence of the human beings, but without any effect. The lady was pestering him to give life to her husband. He said that he would do. He asked the lady to bring a pot of pure water. He said he would exercise his spiritual power into that water. That powered water would have to be drunk by any one of the persons in the family and the dead person would come back to life. But the person who drank that water would die. He asked first the lady to do so. She said," if I left the world, my husband could not manage. He did not even know how to light a gas stove. It would be extremely difficult for him to survive without my presence". She declined. The two children were asked then. Both of them expressed their inability saying that they were very young and they had long miles to go in their life journey. The aged parents of the deceased person when asked said that the person was not the only son for them, they had 3 daughters and two more sons. They had to witness their grand children's marriage etc etc. The spiritual person told the lady" See! Everybody has his or her own desires and wishes. They do not want to come out of that! Probably your husband might not have any such with him. That is why he has left"The lady shut her mouth.

As seen in the above anecdote, attachments are embedded with some kinds of expectations. Real love towards any being or human beings will not have any such bondage.

Man Closer to God

All the nonsense, that we carry inside is not all interested in us. We are only interested in them. we are keeping them together, somehow or the other.

Our Hindu scriptures talk about Six Sins or ***malams,*** as they are called. They are Kama, Krotha, Loba, Moha, Matha, Mathsarya.

Kama is desire, Krotha – anger and hatred, Loba – thinking, to own everything for self. Moha-attachment. Matha – boasting about oneself. Mathsarya – jealousy upon the people above

All these are confined to one word called ego and an equation can be written as,

Man + Ego = God

Or

God – Ego = Man

The purpose of any human life, is to get rid off all the "ego" in the sense, all the six sins, mentioned above and come nearer to God. We should introspect every now and then, so as to move towards that destination.

Bitter Gourd with a Bitter Truth

The purpose of any religious activities or partaking religious rituals is to make the mind purer and try to eliminate the sins one by one. Without that, all those will only be a mere waste.

A Guru was asked by his disciples to accompany them for a pilgrimage to various temples in North. He expressed his inability but instead gave each, a bitter gourd. He instructed them to keep that bitter gourd. with them wherever they go. It should be given back safely to him on their return. They all agreed. On their return, the Guru reminded and got all the pieces. He asked the cook, to prepare a dish with all the pieces and asked to serve to everybody during lunch. He asked all the disciples how the dish tasted. They said, that naturally it would taste only bitter. He questioned how it would be since they had taken them to all the temples. They said the natural taste of the vegetable is bitter it can never change its taste. He said, exactly he wanted to convey only that fact. All the pilgrimage is only a means to end, it can never be an end. The purpose of the pilgrimage, is to make the mind purified, unless it does so, it does not serve any purpose. He also reminded them to ask themselves the question as to whether the pilgrimage had changed them at least to some extent.

This is not a lesson to the disciples alone but to all of us.

Kama, the Root Cause:-

Of all the above six sins, mentioned above, Kama is the basis and will lead to all the other five sins. How?

We will see with an example of the King Ravana from Sri Lanka. He developed Kama, lust towards Sita. So he developed Krotha or hatred towards anybody, who stood as an obstacle to fulfil that. Kama led to Krotha. Hence he thought that Sita should only be belonging to his. Thus he got into Loba. So he developed intense bondage towards Sita. He entered into Moha. Moreover he thought, he was the supreme, whomsoever came to fight against him, he treated them all as inferior. Thus he developed Matha, or ego. Since he could not fulfil his desire of getting the willingness of Sita to marry him, he developed Mathsarya, jealousy towards Rama, the husband of Sita.

So, one single sin, Kama led into the next five sins. This happens in the life of many. Ravana is one example. The desire may be towards a lady, a position in an organisation, a possession of property, house, car or any inanimate thing. If the desires are not able to be fulfilled by one, he will get entangled into the all other sins. That will spoil his mental peace and happiness.

A question may then arise, as to, if all the evil thoughts are the root cause of one's evil, the evil thoughts control man or vice versa. The answer for the question is given by the following anecdote, involving Adi Sankara, the renowned Saint and his disciples:

Adi Sankara was walking through the market place with his disciples. They saw a man dragging a cow by a rope. Sankara told the man to wait and asked his disciples to surround him.

"I am going to teach you something" he continued.

"Tell me who is bound to whom? Is the cow bound to this man or the man is bound to the cow?"

The disciples said without hesitation "Of course the cow is bound to the man!. The man is the master. He is holding the rope. The cow has to follow him, wherever he goes. The man is the master and the cow is the slave."

"Now watch this", said Sankara, got a knife and cut the rope.

The cow ran away from the master and the man ran after his cow. "Look, what is happening", said Sankara

"Do you see who the Master is? The cow is not at all interested in this man. The cow in fact, is trying to escape from this man."

Sankara taught a very sublime lesson to all of us through this incident.

Like the cow, ***All the nonsense, that we carry inside is not all interested in us. We are only interested in them. we are keeping them together, somehow or the other.***

We are going crazy, trying to keep it, all together under our control. The moment we lose interest, in all the garbage filled in our head, and the moment we understand the futility of it, it will start to disappear. Like the cow, it will escape and disappear.

Intense Attachment

We have to free our mind and keep ourselves at peace. But, the bitter truth is that, we are having intense attachments towards inanimate and animate things. The following three incidents will explain the truth:

First One

There was a very rich man in a village. He had gone to some other distant place on a business tour. On his return, he was shocked to see that his house was on intense fire. When many were ready to buy that beautiful house in that village for a very attractive price, he was not ready to sell. Now before his eyes, that house was burning. Many were trying their best, to put off the fire, but it was of no use, since it had spread far and wide, with the heavy wind blowing. He was lamenting heavily" Oh my house! my house!"

At that moment, his eldest son came nearer and said" Why father, you are making a huge cry? Yesterday itself I sold this house for a very very attractive price for a US based NRI. Almost 60% advance also got."

"The much consoled rich man now joined the crowd, witnessing the engulfing fire. Same house same fire, same person. But the grief, he had some moments back, had vanished now.

After a while, his second son came, in very much stressed condition and told him" how father you can be in this free state? We have got only 60% advance. He may or may not give the balance. There is every chance that he may not agree, since the registration process is not yet over"

The rich man again plunged into sorrow and started worrying again for the house only for half an hour. The third son came running towards his father and told joyfully" Father please don't worry. The buyer is such a nice gentle man, who has said to one friend here that he has given the advance, It is as good as his house. Nobody knows that the house will be in fire. So, it would only be fair, if he has to give back the balance amount too"

The rich man again became happy and started dancing and thanking God.

He stared at the burning house, like the others, who were witnessing the fire.

When he thought that it was his house, intense sorrow engulfed him. When he thought, it was not his house, sorrow could not come nearer to him. Nothing is permanent in this world. Nothing belongs to any. All is bound to be destroyed, after some time, or to be owned by some other. This ultimate truth, if remembered well, nothing can affect us

Second One

A famous and very skilled surgeon in a place, before any surgery, used to say "I perform the operation. HE gives life"

At a specific period, his son had to be operated for a major surgery. Can he utter the same words and perform the surgery?. Definitely he won't. Because he has no attachment towards other patients. When it comes to his own son, he has very intimate attachment.

When there is attachment, we have fear of the future. If not, we are fearless and face the future boldly.

Third One

A family of four were travelling in a car to a nearby place on a pilgrimage. Due to heavy rain on the previous night, the roads had become very bad. The call driver, unmindful of the worst condition of the road was riding with high speed. The owner stopped him and told him to go slowly, citing the bad condition of the road and the possible resultant damage to the car.

Next week, for the same place, the same family along with the guests were travelling in a hired car. The owner cum driver of the call taxi was going on the same road, which had not been repaired so far. "Go fast! Why are you going so slow. Already late!" for this question, the driver replied "sorry sir. The roads are very bad. I cannot take risk with my car." The same person who asked his call driver to go slow during last week, was asking now to go fast, since it was not his car. Same way, during last week, driver was trying to go at high speed, since he was not owning the car. This week, the driver was going at a low speed, since he was the owner of the car.

The attachment makes one possessed with the object. That possession drives him into fear and sorrow.

These are the behavious of we, the common men. With the case of the Saints, or very spiritually developed persons, it would be totally different. That happened in the life of Ramana Maharishi, a very renowned Saint. Doctors strongly advised the Saint to go for a major surgery in his arm, or else that cancerous part would affect the whole body. He refused to go for. When his close followers forced him, he agreed, on the condition that he should not be given any anaesthesia. He said that he was not the body. He was not the arm. He was the soul.

While it is not possible for very ordinary people like us to be in the same wave length of the Saint, we should not worry too much about the ailments we undergo. Too much attachment should be shed off.

Without getting rid of all attachments, we cannot move forward in our soul journey. Why?

Get rid off luggages

A prominent temple. Before the temple, an old man would be sitting, selling the requirements of the temple, like beetle leaves, fruits, coconut camphor etc. He would be murmuring "I want to be away from all these worldly affairs. Still the time is not ripe."

One day he told the same thing to a Saint, who came to worship. The Saint immediately told him "Say yes, now! I will take you along with me"

The person said "I too long for it. But, the problem is I have my sons and daughters who are not experienced and yet to be married. If I see them settled, I can start immediately ".

The Saint went out laughingly. Years rolled down. The same place. Same people. "Are you ready now? Come with me" the Saint asked the person.

The person said "I don' t have any other bondage., Children are settled. But I want to see the marriage of my grandsons and granddaughters" The saint left him with a smile. Still more years. Same place. The person was not there. Yet another person was spotted. The Saint enquired about his old friend. The man, looked after the shop, told him "Oh!Are you that person? My father used to tell that he wanted to get rid off all the bondages and go along with you. Last month he passed away suddenly. If he had been alive, he would have come along with you"

The Saint told him" Your father had not gone anywhere else. See that dog! That is your father! He is here only" he clapped his hand

The dog came nearer immediately

The Saint touched its head and asked "Are you ready to come with me at least now?"

"Sorry, I have earned a huge sum of money. I have my own doubt, if my children will take care of all without any problem. That is why I am going around this shop or else the thief will rob my shop"

The Saint remarked "if you are more comfortable with your family luggage, how can you get spirituality? Come out of these"

The lesson by the Saint is to be contemplated especially by older people, since they get entangled into the life struggle, without being able to escape from the clutches of the Samsara Sahara or the **ocean of family circle**. Many think, that the acts towards spiritual practices can be taken later but that ***LATER*** will never come.

Our life cycle has got different stages. In the first stage, young age, we are too young to think about spiritual practices. In the next youth stage, we are too self centred to have the thought about spirituality. After getting married, we are so happy that we do not

have the time to think about that. In our mid career stage, we are so busy that we don't tend to have a thought on that. In the old age, it would be too late to think of it.

This is the curse of Human life.

Procrastination is the thief of not only time in general, but more specifically, the time for our spiritual development.

About Death:-

While this is the fact about spirituality, during different stages, that about death during different stages can also be explained as follows:-

Any resistance comes with changes. Any change has got the following four steps:-

- ***Initial resistance***
- ***Tolerance.***
- ***Acceptance***
- ***Understanding and Appreciation***.

We can illustrate this with death, (the only certainty) as an example.

- *Till we reach 35, we keep ourselves busy to face the practical life. We assume that death is only for others*
- *Between 35 and 50, we begin to bother about our health and we start caring our family health*
- *Between 50 and 65, the fear about death starts haunting us. We prepare ourselves, physically and psychologically for the inevitable – be it our will, our routine medical check up, bank accounts etc*
- *Between 65 and 80, consciously or unconsciously we tend to be spiritualistic. We start accepting that inevitable.*

- *Above 80, we will understand and appreciate the inevitable, since we have understood the reality at that time. This is the beauty of the movie called Life.*

Instead of waiting, till we reach the old age, our scriptures prepare ourselves, to be cognizant of the true nature, right from our young age. We are taught, to balance our life and enjoy every phase of it. Let us live that life from our young age. That is the real and true freedom

Meditation - the Soul Searching Experience

The bottom line is – Vibrate Higher! Meditation aids to vibrate higher!

Time for Self:-

We have seen that, we have to allot time for balancing of five wheels of life-physical, mental, family, career, social. What time one has to allot for himself?That is for meditation.

During prayer, we talk to God. But, during meditation, God will be talking to us. For that we have to do elaborate preparations…

One important preparation is to purify ourselves – bodily and mentally. There are certain requirements to do that, as prescribed in many spiritual practices. Above than the purification of body, purification of mind is of paramount importance. With that, one will come closer to God.

The noted couplet from the world renowned Poet Thiruvalluvar from Tamilnadu reveals the truth, which says that mind purification is of paramount importance. Without that, others will not be of any use, whatever may be the activities they do-going to worship God, doing social service etc. All these activities are the means to purify oneself, but they are not the end in itself.

The physical and mental cleaning should be perfect. Master Choa Kok Sui, the founder of the World Pranic Healing Foundation, has given extensive preparatory measures, before doing meditation. He goes to the extent of saying, unless the purification process is done properly, the effects of meditation will not be realized. In fact the effects will be negative. He quotes the example of applying fertilizer, to the soil for growing plants. If the weeds are not removed, it will also grow with the seeds, through the application of fertilizer. He compares meditation, with the application of fertilizer. By proper purification – both physical and mental and with the purer body and mind, if one does meditation, the effects will be enormous. That will reflect in his personal productivity. That person will be very distinct. from others.

Be Patient:-

The problem with many is, they want to see the benefits of meditation immediately. That depends on so many factors. One should have patience to wait for the benefits.

A story related to a monkey, comes to my mind. A mother monkey asked its younger one, to dig a pit and plant a seed of mango in the soil, close the pit and apply water to the area. The younger one nodded its head. After a month, the mother asked the younger one the feedback. Everything was ok for the mother. But when it was asked how much water, the younger one showed the signs of a larger measure. The mother immediately said in shock, with that measure, the seed would get decayed. The younger one replied-no no – every time I dug the pit out and see if it got decayed. The mother monkey blamed itself for the act of the other.

Most of us are in the mind set of the younger one. We are impatient for results.

The First Prerequisite:-

Another thing about meditation is, irrespective of the quicker and later results, the self purification by the process is more. Meditation makes one person more patient, concentrated and focused.

An anecdote with a grandfather and his grandson will explain this better.

A grandfather living in a village, was in the process of clearing the doubts of his grandson, on meditation. The grandson wanted to do meditation, like his grandfather. But he could not concentrate and do like that of his grandfather. That was his concern. One day, the grandfather asked his grandson, to bring a basket made of palmyra leaves, which will be normally kept at the backyard of the house.(which will contain many pores, through which water may pass through) When the grandson did, the grandfather asked him to take water from the backyard and pour the water into the tub in the bath room. The condition was that, the bath room tub should be filled. The grandson was doing the process several times. Since the basket had many pores, the water got leaked and very little amount of water was poured into the tub. The grandson got much discouraged, disappointed and expressed that to the grandfather.

The grandfather asked him, "what was the colour of the basket initially.?"

"Since it was containing charcoal, it was black" came the reply,.

"How is it after its use?."

"It is very clear" he replied.

"Exactly: like the basket became clear, your mind also will get clearer slowly, through meditation. Please don't look into more benefits now. You will start getting benefits in the long run. At present, do concentrate on sitting calmly, focus for a minute on something. That will do.

The advice by the grandfather to his grandson, is worthy to be applied for us as well.

Meditation-Medical Significance

Human heart very tirelessly works from birth till death. Out of the 7000 litres of blood, pumped every day, 70% of it goes to brain, the rest 30% to the remaining body.

How is this possible?

Heart follows a time discipline, as set by God. In normal conditions, the heart takes 0.3 seconds to contract (systolic) and 0.5 seconds to relax (diastolic).

Hence, 0.3 + 0.5 = 0.8 seconds are required by the heart to complete one beat (1 cardiac cycle)

That means in 1 min, the heart beats roughly 72 times, which is considered as normal heart beat.

With 0.5 secs for relaxing phase, the blood becomes 100% pure.

In some stressful conditions, the body demands more blood in less time and in this situation the heart reduces the relaxing period of 0.5 seconds to 0.4 seconds. Thus, in this case, the heart beats 82 times in 1 minute and only 80% of blood gets purified.

On more and more demand, the relaxing time is further reduced to 0.3 seconds, at that period only 60% of blood is purified.

Imagine the consequences of the lesser oxygenated blood, circulating in our arteries.

Deep Breathing is the key to ensure better Oxygenation of the blood.

Factors responsible for the activity of the brain:

1. 25% – 30% is due to the Diet, we consume.
2. 70% – 75% is due to the emotions, attitude, memories and other processes of the brain.

Thus, to calm the brain and reduce the demand on the heart to pump more and more blood, brain needs to be given a rest.

Meditation is the most useful tool to calm an agitated mind.

When we sit with eyes closed and meditate, the brain gets calmer, heart gets rested, thus insulating us from the diseases of heart and brain.

More over, meditation is one way to ward off many ailments. How?

VIBRATE HIGHER!

One of my spiritual friends, who himself is a doctor, gave some interesting facts about vibrations, from health point of view:-

The covid virus has a vibration of 5.5 hz and dies above 25.5 hz. For humans with a higher vibration, infection is a minor irritant and virus is soon eliminated.

The following negative qualities, will lead to low vibration:-

- *Fear, Phobia, Suspicion*
- *Anxiety, Stress, Tension.*
- *Jealousy, Anger, Rage*
- *Hate, Greed*
- *Attachment or Pain*

The point to remember is, we have to vibrate higher, so that our immune system is protected.

The frequency of the earth today is 27.4 hz., but there are places that vibrate very low like:-

- *Hospitals*
- *Assistance Centers*
- *Jails*
- *Underground etc.*

It is where the vibration drops to 20hz, or less. For humans with low vibration, the virus becomes dangerous.

- *Pain 0.1 to 2 hz.*
- *Fear 0.2 to 2.2 hz.*
- *Irritation 0.9 to 6.8 hz.*
- *Noise 0.6 to 2.2 hz.*
- Worries 0.8 hz.
- Ego 1.9 hz.

A higher vibration, on the other hand, is the outcome of the following behaviour:-

- Generosity 95hz
- Gratitude 150 hz
- Love and Compassion 150 hz or more.
- Unconditional and universal love 205hz

So, the bottom line is, ***Vibrate Higher! Meditation is one, that aids to vibrate higher!***

Parikarams:-

Many will think that meditation will remove our sins and it is the panacea to ward off our evils. Is it true? Let us go deeper on this:-

We have heard the following statements in Indian culture:-

We have done all the parikarams (compensation for the committed sins, done in the fast.) as per the astrologer's predictions. Nothing happened. We don't know what to do.

For those people, this story:-

A king, who went for hunting in a forest, found that it had become very dark and he planned to return to his kingdom. At that moment, he could spot an animal in a branch of a tree. Assuming it, as a wild animal, he aimed his arrow, towards it. Immediately he heard a lamenting voice "Ah!. I am finished"

Realising that it was the voice of a human being, he went nearer to the place. To his utter shock, it was a youth, killed by his arrow. Without leaving the place, he ordered his people, to find out, if the parents of the deceased could be traced.

They went on a frantic search and finally they brought a blind old couple, whose family was said to have survived, by cutting the trees in the forest, for which job, the youth had been engaged. The king pleaded with them that it was not done intentionally, but he accidentally killed him, thinking as a wild animal. Sensing that they were not convinced, he called his people to bring two plates-one for a sword, around his waist, and another with full of gold coins. After they brought, he took all the valuables worn by him and added to the gold coins.

He went flat to their feet and told them that he was the culprit, who instead of taking care of his citizens, killed one, that too, a youth who had to support his old blind parents.

He also told them that anything in this world could not compensate the murder, but he put forth two options, to the old people:

They could take the entire gold and priceless ornaments, with which they could live, without anybody's help. If they were not interested, they could kill the king, for which they could employ the sword, kept in the other plate,

He went down to the feet of the couple, disrobing his crown. All were awe struck, thinking what would happen.

After a moment the old man started talking "I have thought of these two options. After my dear young son's death, what am I going to do with these gold?" when he gave a pause, all started guessing that the old man would be going to kill the king. All stood, with killing silence. The king sat unperturbed.

The old man continued" As you suppose, Iam not going to kill your king. These valuables are nothing, before the life of my only young son. The repentance by the King for the grave mistake committed, touched my wounded heart. He was ready to offer his life. The tears shed by the king, made me moved. That will suffice. I don't want the people of this kingdom to suffer, by the loss of this noble king. By that killing, my son in no way will come back to life. Even my son's soul will not forgive me for that."

With these words, he started from the spot, without bothering about anybody.

All were astonished to note the wisdom from that ordinary wood cutter.

We are all like the king. The sins we are committing are like the murder. The wood cutter is GOD. We should understand that God does not want the flamboyant compensations, we are giving to him in different forms. These compensations are only means to end and they are not the end. Without proper understanding, we do a lot of things to compensate for the sins, committed. We cannot expect that God will have to accept the things, which we think, will please him. What HE wants is the total acceptance of our mistakes, committed consciously or unconsciously, in this or previous births. If we totally surrender to HIM, he will definitely forgive us. If one does this inner purification, then the meditation done after that, will have fruitful results. Without that, it will not have any effect at all. Purification of mind and body are the prerequisites for any meditation.

There is a belief that renowned Saints can change the fate of some people. People used to go to temples to pray to God to reduce their sins or at least to reduce their sufferings. Many approach the Saints for the purpose. The question is, can they change their total fate? Excepting a very very few Saints, others cannot. But, the way we perceive the sufferings, they can change. Suppose you have 5000 INR as the coins with you It is very difficult to carry the entire coins. But somebody takes that and gives you 2 X 2000 plus 2 x 500 currency notes, you wont feel the pinch. This is what the renowned Saints do. They prepare us to accept the sufferings, as the karmic debt and make us matured to reconcile, which makes our sufferings to be felt lighter. Like that of the person, who feels the difference between 5000INR as the currency and the whole lot of coins, the same karmic debt can be felt in a different way. If we approach those Saints, they can prepare us for facing the problems or the sufferings

MEDITATION – THE KEY TO REAL HEALING

How it is to be done? Advice by Ramana Maharishi will be handy to us:

A school boy had a doubt for quite a long time. His parents could not clear that doubt. One day when all the three had been to have Dharshan with Bhagwan Ramana Maharishi, he came out with that doubt to the MaharishiWhat is Dhyanam?(Meditation), the boy asked the Maharishi.

Maharishi with a laughter asked the attendants to serve a dosa to the boy.

Maharishi told the boy, to start eating the dosa, as soon as the signal had come from him. Also he should stop, as soon as the second signal had come from him. The boy was enthused. Others got confused. The boy was awaiting the signal, with his hand on the dosa. Maharishi made him wait for some time and then only he gave the signal. The boy hurriedly took pieces of dosa and started thrusting into his mouth, simultaneously keeping an eye on the Maharishi's face, awaiting the second signal. The dosa had become a very small piece then. The boy had been patiently awaiting the signal.

The time was passing by. The boy had been patiently awaiting the signal. Others were also closely watching the scene. The second signal came at an unexpected moment and the boy put the last piece into his mouth.

Maharishi with a smile on his face, told the boy "As you had your entire attention on me and the dosa, between the two signals: if you have your full rapt attention to God, that is Dhyanam. Do you understand?" Not only the boy, we also got the right answer.

The two signals mentioned by Ramana Maharishi are:-

1. **Life**
2. **Death**

Our attention should be towards God on all occasions in our life starting from cradle to grave. That was the message given by Maharishi.

But, in reality many unmindful of the above precious advice do all sorts of evils in our life and finally, during our end, while admitted in an ICU, realise our grave sins and utter,

"O! Lord! I could see you only now"

God would say smilingly "I also see you now"

Both are in 'I… C… U.' mode.

Why this late realisation? Why not earlier?

In that life journey, to make it Peaceful and Blissful, it would be worthwhile, if we follow these Laws of Karma:-

Eight Laws of Karma

1. *Whatever we do in this universe, will come back to us*
2. *Nothing happens to us as such, we only have done those necessary for us*
3. *Change will happen, only if we accept certain things*
4. *When we change ourselves, our life follows the change and it will also change*
5. *We only are responsible for whatever happens to us*

6. *Yesterday today tomorrow – all the three are inter related*
7. *We cannot think of two different things at the same time*
8. *Our character should refelect our thoughts and actions*

Cool Lessons from an Earthern Pot

Once an earthern pot was asked, how it was able to maintain coolness, both inside and outside, in spite of the intense heat outside.

It replied "I know fully, my beginning and end – that I came from sand and will go to sand itself. As the one who fully realises this fact, why should I turn hot?"

The above advice from the pot is worthy to be followed in letter and spirit.

Our journey of life is short. Why ego? Follow the attitude of gratitude to those who have done good for us, follow the spirit of forgiveness, with those, whom we think, have done bad to us.

Jayam or Vijayam?

The original name given by Sage Vyasa to the Epic Mahabharatha, was Jayam, to conquer. Which is to be conqured – lost Kingdom? Wealth? – NO! To conquer one self, against all the evils. Even Yudhishtra could not, when he was allowed, to enter the heaven, with the dog. He could not digest, his cousins, Kaurava being in heaven. When he was told, that they died in the war, hence they had come for spending some time in heaven: to go back to the earth, to be born again. He got ashamed. He went to river Ganges and repented for his jealousy. Then only, he got Moksha. That is the last episode of Mahabharatha. While this is the case of highly developed soul, like Yudhishtra, what about us, very ordinary people? In each and every part of our human life, we have to conquer evil, in us and get the final victory of attaining Moksha, the liberation from birth. That will be, should be, the purpose of all spiritual practices.

Old is Gold

In each and every part of our life, if we have the following motto as given in our ancient scriptures,

Vasudeva Kudumbagam

and the saying in ancient Tamil, by the poet Kanian Poonkunranaar,

Yaathum Oore, yaavarum Kelir, meaning the whole world is one and all are our own people.

In that case, Our life mission will become the following:-

I won't lament why I have been born. But, will take a resolution, today itself - "Iam not going to take any more births, by my conviction to do righteous actions"

That is indeed, the true spirit of spirituality

To Conclude:-

We have seen, in more detail, how to balance the Six Wheels of our life-Physical, Mental, Family, Career, Social, Spiritual.

I was able to watch the U tube video, by Swami Gyanvatsal, wherein he has very nicely and vividly explained, how our 24 hours of life have to be spent, for a balanced way of leading our life. He calls that as the balance sheet of life, which is given for our easy reference:-

Balance Sheet of Life:-

- ***8-hrs-for wealth through honest profession***
- ***8 hrs – for sleep and rest – for our body battery Charge***
- ***8 hrs for 3H , 3F and 3S***
- ***3 H – Health, hygiene, hobby – Deviation***
- ***3 F – Family, friend and faith – Relationship***

- ***3S – Service, Soul, Smile – Eternal satisfaction***

Let us follow the above principles very scrupulously to have a Blissful and Peaceful Life!

Let God be with us in all our endeavours!

Reflections:-

Reflections:-

BLISS & PEACE PROGRAM

Episode - 61 (03-09-2022)

(Concluding part of the Whole programme)

Time : **Every Saturday 5.00 pm to 5.30 pm**

Speaker :

Shri. M.Harihara Mahadevan

Corporate Trainer & HR Faculty

Topic :

தொட்டு விடும் தூரமே...

Organized by :

The 1234 Foundation
Rotary Club of Virudhunagar Idhayam
Readers Club, CAS Institute
Amar Seva Sangam

Broadcast by :

tamerica.TV

த merica TV

1st Tamil Channel from America

Meeting ID : 833 0197 4319
Passcode : 1234

தவறவிடும் வாய்ப்பல்ல இது!

Webinar

International Tamil University Award

Photo taken on the occasion of the Award presented to M.Harihara Mahadevan for his book in Tamil entitled Num Ilakkukalai Nokki Payanippom by International Tamil University USA on 18th March at Music Academy.

Award given by Dr. Selvin Kumar, Founder/President of the University. M/S. Ravi Tamil Vanan, MD Manimekalai Prasuram and M/S Prakasam and Indran from Karnataka look on.

With Participants of a Training program

www.ingramcontent.com/pod-product-compliance
Lightning Source LLC
LaVergne TN
LVHW041156150826
845673LV00001B/187

* 9 7 9 8 8 9 0 2 6 7 4 2 9 *